LEGAL MARKETING
STRAIGHT TALK

— PRESENTS —

SOLVING THE PUZZLE

Online Marketing for Attorneys

STEVEN LONG
WITH JESSICA AINSWORTH

Solving the Puzzle - Online Marketing for Attorneys
Copyright © 2021 by Steven Long and Jessica Ainsworth

Author Photograph for Steve by
          Precision Legal Marketing Steven Long ;)

Author photo by Todd I. Mason, Jr.,
          Capture Essence Photography

Cover Design by 100 Covers

Formatting & Typesetting by Black Bee Media

ISBN: 978-1-7367525-2-4 (Hardcover)

       978-1-7367525-1-7 (Paperback)

       978-1-7367525-0-0 (Ebook)

Download Your FREE Gifts

We are committed to making sure that you are prepared for the realm of legal marketing. As such, to go along with this book, we have put together a collection of free resources to help you implement your law firm's marketing strategy.

Download your FREE resources here:

http://legalmarketingstraighttalk.com

Table of Contents

Part 4
Content Marketing

Part 5
Social Media

Part 6
Advertising

Part 7

BONUS

Part 1:

Getting Started

The Blueprint of Law Firm Marketing

A pivotal part of running and managing your law firm means learning how to run a business. It can often get overwhelming, and for a good reason – after all, in law school, you are typically taught law and not the fundamentals of running your firm.

To run a successful law firm, you first need to become an expert at, among other things, client intake, managing an office, bookkeeping, and, most importantly, *legal marketing*.

Knowing how to market your law firm is unarguably one of the most critical skills you require to make your firm untouched heights and successful. Understanding all that goes with it can also help keep you safe from those who may be looking to take advantage of you.

To get started with marketing your law firm, you must have a concrete plan, some digital marketing tools, and some business know-how.

This book is meant to cover the basics of marketing your firm. While there is a ton of practical information and advice within these pages, understand that this book could be 5 times its size if it contained all of the needed nonsensical information. This is not a book that promises to double your lead count if you follow some advanced techniques. That is not what this is about. This is meant to be foundational learning to build onto; a launch pad if you will. It's a starting point. It will empower you to sniff out bullshit from unscrupulous marketers trying to sell you XYZ.

You will also notice we use words like "customers", "advertising" and "business" in this book. It's purposeful. We want you thinking like a business owner and not necessarily like an attorney. You have that covered. Don't worry, there is no "click funnel link black hat voodoo" whatever present in this book. Just straightforward information.

As with your chosen discipline of the law, marketing is a highly specialized endeavour. Legal marketing itself is an animal unto itself. While there are some actionable DIY tips in this book, please feel free to hire a professional using this as your basic blueprint. We don't pander much here, but feel free to call us at Precision Legal Marketing for any level of advice or questions you may have after reading these pages.

With that...let's get into it.

11 Digital Basic Marketing Tools for Lawyers

Starting anything new can feel overwhelming, but it is vital to understand that as your law practice grows, it's imperative that you differentiate your firm from the other players present in the already oversaturated legal market.

Remember, successful marketing can help your firm to stand out from the competition and, thus, will attract new clients to your practice. Let's start with some useful digital marketing tools for lawyers that you must incorporate in your marketing strategy:

#1: Build an appealing website for your firm

Mostly, the first impression of people about you and your firm will be received through your website. Therefore, you must ensure that it represents your firm's reputation, ideologies and what it stands for clearly.

Moreover, make sure that it's responsive, fast, secure, and well-designed.

When you are building the website, ensure that it at least contains an "About Us" page that shares your story, tells why you exist and why you are better than other attorneys in the market. Additionally, add a page that lists your mission and values, a list of all the firm's services, client testimonials, case studies, blogs, and even a FAQ, among other pages. This is a bare minimum requirement. While we of course design and build stunning future proof websites, you won't hurt my feelings if you head off to squarespace or one of the other drag and drop DIY tools to get yourself started.

#2: Get discovered online through search engine optimization (SEO)

You can build the most incredible website or blog page but making sure that the target audience discovers your website/blog page is all that truly matters. To help you achieve that, this is where search engine optimization (SEO) comes into play. SEO is a crucial component of any effective digital marketing strategy for law firms.

At its core, SEO produces and directs traffic to your website by allowing visitors to easily locate your firm when surfing online. The better your site's SEO is, the better it'll be ranked by search engines, which means that your firms' website will appear higher in search results.

For this purpose, you can hire expert SEO professionals (such as Precision Legal Marketing - shameless plug) who can help you reach your true potential.

#3: Generate traffic with the help of blogging and guest blogging

Blogging is yet another excellent way to generate and draw traffic to your firm's website. Search topics your target audience would be interested in and hire experienced writers to produce appealing blog posts on them.

In addition, guest blogging is also a good way to increase traffic. To begin, make a list of blogs you would be interested in a guest post on, check out their guest-blogging policy, and then apply.

To amplify your probabilities of getting published, where feasible, first try to build an amicable relationship with the organization, research and note down post ideas, go through the publication's guest posting policies, and then pitch your idea.

#4: Share accomplishments with masses through a press release

Press releases are an excellent way to spread and share any noteworthy information and accomplishments linked to your law firm. Whether it is a case you have nailed or any new partnerships built – issuing a press release can work great to spread the news.

Remember, they don't supersede full-scale PR outreach to journalists but can effectively and quickly get your story out among the masses.

It's essential to keep in mind that journalists tend to disregard and even obliterate press releases that specifically don't offer them something or if they feel it's not newsworthy and/or of any interest to the readers. Therefore, always make sure to review and see if the news you want to publish is interesting or not.

#5: Augment connections with the help of email marketing

Email marketing is still one of the essential communication tools in digital marketing for lawyers. Emailing is a great way to keep your company in front-of-mind among present and present clients and also to capture new business.

A monthly or weekly newsletter is a decent way to stay in touch with subscribers. Law firms that focus on sending out valuable, relevant, and personalized emails generally perform better than those who don't.

#6: Bolster audience networks with content marketing

High quality and relevant content that encourages dialogue with your target audience will ultimately deepen and strengthen your relationship and will also lead to more business. However, you must know that content marketing is more than your law firm's blog.

When executed correctly, it involves guides, articles, eBooks, quizzes, webinars, podcasts, videos, etc. These content formats can be potent growth drivers for your firm. Just be sure to focus on generating timely, thoughtful, and educational content that is tailored particularly for your audience and is of high quality.

#7: Take advantage of social media marketing

Today, cultivating an alluring image through social media is an essential part of public relations and digital marketing for any law firm. Social media platforms such as Facebook, Twitter, and Instagram should be used to build your law firms' brand, connect with your target audience, drive website traffic, and generate more leads.

Social media marketing involves publishing high-quality content - that can be repurposed from your site - on your social media profiles, analyzing your results, engaging and listening to your followers, and running paid social media advertisements. Moreover, do not forget to build a professional social media profile bio as it's usually viewed more than any other content you share.

#8: Boost traffic and generate leads through video marketing

Video marketing fills all the boxes if you want to create more traffic, generate more leads, and acquire more clients for your law firm. It can help you to improve engagement with the target audience, improve your SEO and search rankings, and persuade prospective clients that you are the right firm for their job.

In video marketing, you can create vlogs, conduct interviews with lawyers, develop a case study or customer testimonial videos to build trust and social proof, create educational content that emphasizes particular questions asked by clients, and so much more.

#9: Advertise your law firm to create awareness and brand credibility

Both paid and unpaid advertising endeavors are excellent ways of creating awareness about your brand. Organic advertisements can be done via customer testimonials, reviews, etc. Whereas paid can be achieved through PPC, i.e., pay per click.

PPC are online ads that you pay for when someone clicks on them. The most popular example of this is Google AdWords; they are the ads you see at the top of the Google search engine. A critical thing to note with PPC or any ads you post online or send in an email newsletter is that they must always take the receiver to a designated landing page that's particular to the ad you're using.

For example, in email marketing, your landing page must reflect what your ad offered. If the ad was for real estate planning services, then the landing page should talk about the services you offer in that field.

#10: List your firm in a legal directory to enhance website SEO

Another easy way augments your site's SEO through link building is via listing your firm in a legal directory. You can get yourself registered in more than one but keep in mind that some are free while others charge a fee for the registration.

#11: Hire marketing professionals for reputation management

There's no denying that bad days can come along anytime, anywhere, and unannounced. So, it is always better to be safe than sorry later. Digital marketing professionals can help you build and manage the reputation of your law firm. God forbid, if the firm is ever going through a rough phase, you can count on the professionals to clean up the mess and keep your reputation intact.

There's a lot of terminology in here that may be confusing, but don't worry we go into all of this and more throughout the book. So, stay tuned!

However, before we get that far, let's first look to narrow down exactly *who* your target audience is.

Defining Your Target Audience

Not everyone can be your client.

"Why do I need to define an audience?"

The answer is simple. In order to lead a successful marketing campaign, you have to understand who you're marketing to - and the legal industry is no different. Knowing who your target audience is can help determine where the best place to market to them is, improve your results and knowing this could save you big bucks!

Due to Covid in mid-March of 2020, many states had issued executive orders closing non-essential businesses and ordering a shelter in place. Business owners were swept up in the whirlwind of everything wondering how their business would survive an extended closure. Without clients, how could they pay their employees who were depending on the income? Without generating revenue, would they even be able to pay their rent for their office(s)?

Many law firms (and businesses in general) turned to finding creative ways to stay afloat. Quite a few of those law firms and businesses had turned to advertising on social media to let their potential clients know that they were still open and to promote certain practice areas that had become more relevant during the time, such as divorce, child custody, estate planning, etc. However, without a clear idea of who their target audience is, it's easy to target the wrong people.

Here's why ensuring that you're producing content geared at your law firm's target audience is important... If you're paying to advertise to the wider audience just to boost engagements and build a following, those people are not likely to convert to clients. Not only is this a waste of your money, but it also affects the algorithm for advertising campaigns on the whole. That last part is especially important if you're using tracking for retargeting purposes through Google Ads or the Facebook Pixel (and you should be). Those unqualified leads are then captured in your spider web and you'll continue wasting your money on any retargeting efforts. And who has money to waste during times of uncertainty?

The more you understand just who your target audience is as well, the more you'll understand where your ideal clients are and the kind of content that will resonate better with them. And finally, people who are not in your target audience may end up contracting your firm or seeking out consultations. In fact, you can still "sell" to them. Your target audience revolves around those who are *most* likely to make a purchase and therefore, are your *targeted* audience.

All right. Enough about *why* defining your target audience is important. Now onto *how* you can define your target audience. As we go through this, please keep in mind that it's always a good practice to periodically check to ensure your target audience remains the same. COVID-19 presented volatile, unprecedented times that will have lasting impact. Consumer behaviors have changed drastically after the pandemic took us by storm. In 2008, the economy was rocked by the housing market and ensuing stock market crash and subsequent recession. These major events should force business owners to take a look at their target audience as it may change at a rapid pace and continue to evolve as the economy recovers. Where one practice area may have been more relevant pre-COVID, may now be thrown off kilter as a result of the pandemic.

That's right ladies and gentlemen, you can't escape economics.

So, *how* do we define our target audiences. Many law firm business owners make the mistake of following their gut instinct and not doing the research. With a little bit of research on your audience, you'll find a higher return on investment (ROI) on your marketing efforts. What should you be researching? It's tempting to come in with a group of people that you'd *like* to market to, but that's not always the right answer. Let's start by looking at your current clients. That may be easier said than done for those who have been in business for a little while. Those just starting out should take a look at their closest competitors.

Use this list as a starting point to help you determine commonalities in your current customers:

- Age
- Location
- Language
- Spending Power
- Jobs/Careers/Positions
- Interests
- Stage of Life

Not all of those demographics will be relevant to your law firm/practice area. For instance, those practicing family law are going to be targeting a completely different target audience to those practicing real estate law. However, there may be some overlapping traits in there as well. A family law firm that specializes in divorce and child custody will have massive overlap with estate planning and other family law matters, all the while searching for those divorce retainers.

Age will be relevant for most practice areas, if not all. A divorce lawyer is not going to be targeting minors - or likely even those between 18 - 25. We're not saying that adults between the ages of 18 - 25 aren't going to be looking for a divorce lawyer. What we're saying is that the average age of those seeking divorces is typically higher and therefore, **that age group would be excluded from their target audience.** Converley Personal Injury attorneys don't necessarily care what age their clients are. Though someone focussed on nursing home abuse cases certainly would.

Many law firms offer their services to clients within specific geographic regions. Even for those whose clients come from various locations, you likely have higher concentrations of clients in particular areas.

Have you ever heard some people say "You know what the word assume means, right? It means to make an A$$ out of U and ME." Well, language is an area that many (including myself at one point) have a common misconception that if you're in the U.S. they speak English. We are a melting pot of diversity. Assuming that your target audience all speaks English is wrong. This is why research is so important.

Spending power and ultimately income are areas that some law firms will need to take into account. A lower income level means that they may not have as large of a disposable income. It doesn't mean that they should be excluded from your target audience if they are your most likely client. Again, we come back to relevance for practice areas.

Jobs/Careers/Positions, another demographic that may not be as relevant for every business. However, for those practicing in commercial real estate, employment law, etc., this demographic can be the key.

What do your customers like to do (aside from enjoy your products and services)? What other businesses do they frequent or follow on social media? We're not telling you to go out there and stalk your clients, but knowing this can help you further define where you should be marketing to your target audience as well as what kind of content may resonate better with them.

Finally, we come to the stage of life demographic. Are your customers likely to be college students? New parents? Getting ready to retire? Already retired? Are you marketing to the elderly who may be in need of a will or estate plan? Are you marketing to families looking to adopt?

Where can you get much of this information? Why, the US Census Bureau of course. Wikipedia pages are also a decent source of some of this information, especially in well defined rural areas.

Yet another useful way to help determine your target audience is by looking at the insights of your social media business pages. They all offer an "insights" tab that show you the numbers and analytics behind your page. How active is your page? Have you acquired any new followers? Who is interacting and engaging with your page?

Knowing this information can help you fill in the knowledge gaps to further refine your audience.

Now, we briefly mentioned a little earlier that conducting a competitor analysis can help you identify your potential clients as well. Using those same guidelines, we talked about above, have a look at who your competitors are targeting and who their current clients are. Innovation can help set you apart, but knowing what's already working and what's not can provide some much-needed information to get you started. The caveat here is that you won't be able to get a detailed analysis on your competitors' clients and those interacting with their social pages, but again, it's a good jumping off point.

Make a statement. While we won't go into how to write a brand positioning statement in this book, you should consider making a statement which will define your target audience. Take a look at some of your favorite brand's positioning statements. We'll look at Nike's brand positioning statement for example:

"For serious athletes, Nike gives confidence that provides the perfect shoe for every sport."

Phil Knight and Bill Bowerman, the founders of the Nike brand, were they themselves athletes who had recognized a hole in the market. Bill Bowerman, a famous track and field coach set out to increase running speed by decreasing the weight of the shoe.

"A shoe must be three things; It must be light, comfortable, and it's got to go the distance." - Bill Bowerman.

They developed their brand with a target audience in mind, but their brand has evolved into more than just producing shoes for runners. What did you notice about their positioning statement? They've identified their target audience as being serious athletes, so that even non-athletes will identify with Nike's products.

Some final advice on establishing your target audience is this: Be willing to make mistakes. Nothing is ever really cut and dry. You're going to make mistakes; We all make mistakes - even this author. Don't get hung up on one particular idea. If something isn't working, remain flexible and open minded until you find what resonates with your target audience. That said, this doesn't mean you need to pivot your marketing mission every other month.

You always have the option to do some A/B split testing to determine what wording or what images may invoke a stronger response from your target audience, but it all starts with defining exactly *who* you're targeting.

Are you ready to take the next step? Let's look at websites....

Part 2:

Websites

Unboxing Law Firm Websites

Websites are a major part of a law firm's success in the digital sphere. They are the digital face of your organization. And in the age of information and online reputation, your law firm's website presence can impact your bottom line in many ways. How? Let's take a look at how a typical client may find your firm...

First, they will search online (mostly on mobile devices) to find any local firms that cater to their needs.

Potential new clients tend to do their due diligence when choosing legal services or an attorney to work with. In most cases, it is not something most people search for every day, and it can be quite nerve racking even thinking about meeting with a lawyer. So, having a professional web presence that showcases your firm's expertise and ability is extremely important. Some clients may even be referred to your firm, but may never reach out to you because they couldn't find you online.

Secondly, what they find when they do see your firm's website says a lot about you – and your firm. Does your website represent you and your firm's reputation?

So, let's now look at what they may find in terms of your website, and see why we believe Lawyers should be practicing law – and not spending their time designing and maintaining their own websites.

Of course there are some do-it-yourself options available like Wix, Squarespace or WordPress. Or, you can hire a local web designer or a legal-focused <u>Internet Marketing Agency</u> (Like Precision Legal Marketing - yup, no shame).

So, let's take a look at the top 5 reasons law firms should not be designing and maintaining their own websites:

5 Reasons Law Firms Should Not Be Designing and Maintaining their Own Websites

1. Do-It-Yourself sites like WIX and Squarespace and other similar FREE platforms typically don't work well for Law Firms

Sure, these platforms are quick to set-up a site for your office, but tend not to be the best option when trying to market your efforts. Would you recommend a client to a cheap doctor or refer to a cheap lawyer?

The reality is these platforms are designed for a small business that is just starting out and needs something simple. This is fine if you just want to have a small website up to say, "Hey, we're here." You may be thinking, hey that's me, I'm just starting out.

The challenge with these platforms is that they typically aren't search engine friendly. This means that your small website gets lost within the noise of millions of other businesses and law firms. We're sure you'd rather stand out and have site architecture set-up to help market your firm to the world, and not just have a web page that gets lost in the crowd. We will cover <u>SEO</u> in more detail in a later chapter, but for now all you need to know is that it is a long term investment in the position of your website on a search engine.

2. Small or low-cost hosting plans tend to have their own set of pitfalls

These plans often have little to no site security, which increases the amount of spam that you may receive both on the website and also in your email inbox. With a lack of proper site security and an increase in spam, this also slows down a website's ability to load quickly on a browser.

Slow sites rank poorly with search engines, which doesn't help the bottom line of your business as it doesn't help potential clients find you. In fact, Google has launched a whole host of tools for looking at site load speed and how to make your site load faster. If it is important to Google, it should be important to you too. Remember, 78% of all searches are done at Google.

3. Site Security may be Insufficient

It is imperative that your law firm's website is secure. A simple appearance of having HTTPS as part of your site's URL not only brings security, but also credibility to your clients, to social media outlets, as well as search engines. Google has started to display a warning to potential visitors if a site isn't secure. Once this warning is seen, it is difficult to get that potential client to return.

HTTPS can often be difficult to install and debug, but it is a must have.

4. WordPress and Plugins

WordPress is one of the most popular Content Management Platforms being utilized by millions of businesses worldwide. This platform is one of the most robust on the market. It is extremely Search Engine Friendly, when built right, and allows for an ever increasing level of customizations.

It's very tempting for a Law Firm to build a site utilizing WordPress, and knowing how to navigate this platform oftentimes requires experienced web designers to create the desired user experience.

Each component of a word press site has to be carefully considered for its functionality as well as its overall design to enhance a visitors user experience. The most common components of WordPress sites are called themes (what makes the sites look the way it does) and plugins (which ads functionality to a site).

There are some serious items to consider when adding templates and themes and plugins...

What you may not know is that not all plugins work with all themes, and visa versa. Also, not all plugins work together either. Also, plugins are the leading source of website hacks and other nefarious activities that can affect your site. We have seen entire websites taken down by a single plugin someone installed.

Because each plugin and theme is authored by anyone who has the ability to code, there are several potential challenges in terms of making sure all of the components are compatible. Also, WordPress improves it's platform, each theme and plugin also has to be upgraded regularly.

Upgrades to the WordPress platform and to the various themes and plugins may lead to a component becoming outdated, or even worse, have the potential for your site to be hacked.

Having an experienced team manage your Law Firms websites allows the liability to rest on your team, and not on you. This allows you to focus more on your clients, where really your efforts should be, right?

5. Time is Money, and Your Time is Valuable

Let's be honest here, if you have enough free time to build your own site – maybe you should consider the root cause of your free time – not enough clients.

Sure you can spend your free time learning <u>web design</u> and <u>Search Engine Optimization</u> that isn't a bad thing (we love this stuff), but we want you to do what you do best, be a lawyer.

At this point, you may be wondering just what it may cost to build your website. Let's take a look at that.

Elements of a Successful Website for Law Firms

Are you confused about what makes up a website for a law firm successful? And want to learn how to develop a successful law firm website for your practice?

Then, you've come to the right chapter!

The truth of the matter is that there are particular elements that every successful law firm website has in common. In this chapter, we'll discuss what your law firm website needs to attract more clients and make it successful.

But first, let's understand why it's so important to have a decent looking website and what it can mean to your business.

Why Is It Essential to Design a Successful Website for Law Firms?

Imagine that you are a client, driving to meet an attorney for the first time. You reach their office and see that it is located in a seedy-looking and run-down building. The brick siding looks like it caught fire at one point and the windows are a shade of hazy not seen since 1977. As you enter through the dingy and smudged glass door, you notice that the pavement out front is cracked, and the paint in the entrance hall is peeling due to water or sewage.

Inside, it looks like the furniture was salvaged curbside, and the plants in the corner are on their deathbed. Some light bulbs above your head are flickering, with flies fluttering around.

In this instance, you're screaming in your head: *Would a respected and competent lawyer work in an office like this? Why would I hire this person?* You leave! Quickly I might add.

Likewise, if your website is poorly designed, out-of-date, and missing essential elements, you are providing every prospective client on the web the digital counterpart of this depressing, run-down office tour — and let's not forget that it is their first impression of you!

So, why should you settle for an outdated and inferior website when you would never let your office languish in a similar fashion?

Elements of a Successful Law Firm Website

Remember that it's always going to be particularly tough for up-and-coming and smaller law firms to compete with the massive, successful firms in their areas. But there are ways to give your competitors some stiff competition.

One effective way to do it is to optimize your site for organic search as it'll allow more leads to find you online, and site architecture plays an integral role in accomplishing that. More on this can be found in the chapter that covers SEO.

Keep in mind that law firms are service-based businesses. Therefore, instead of creating a plethora of product pages with mere descriptions, your website must ideally feature:

- A homepage
- A blog
- A contact page
- As many primary service pages as you require to describe what your firm does

- An 'about us' section where you profess your firm's mission statement, values, and profiles of your attorneys

These are the critical elements of a successful law firm site, but how should you structure and link them on the website itself?

Read ahead to learn how it's done. And the better you do at establishing the below, the better success you can expect long term on the web.

Before you make another move, go to a search engine and type "best lawyer in…" your town or city. Take a look around some of the other sites online. Note what you like and don't like. Look in other large AND small metros across the country and do the same.

1. Focus on the homepage contents user experience

The homepage of your site is a logical place to start when you want to design an effective site architecture. The homepage of your law firm should convey a great deal of information all at once. It must display what your practice is about visually and in text, what legal areas your practice covers, and how much former clients trust your services. It should also be very easy to navigate and present this information in a very easy to understand way. Sounds ambiguous doesn't it?

So, how is this accomplished? Here are the nuts and bolts with some jargon you probably haven't heard before. We left this in place here so that you can use this to fact check a vendor you may be considering to build your site. We have located a glossary of terms for reference in the back of this book. So, there is no better time to dig in like right now.

Competitive keywords

First, your site homepage should use competitive legal keywords. For example, 'chapter 7 bankruptcy attorney Milwaukee' illustrates high competition and receives only ten searches every month in Google's Keyword Planner. The trick though is to not splash this all over the page. You need to weave these terms into the text and design of your home page. You will want to use specific text in specific places. The easiest way to think about this is: pretend you are designing the front page of the New York Times. You have the masthead, the sub headings and the body text of each article.

So, use such competitive keywords in your H1, H2s, and meta tags. What are these? See the SEO chapter.

Past client reviews

Remember that you're a service-based business that heavily relies on past client reviews to attain traction in your area.

Thus, you must designate a chunk of your homepage to showcase five-star customer reviews with brief praises about your legal services. Such reviews will help you to bolster trust among visitors to your website. Don't have any reviews? GO GET SOME TODAY! Call your past happy clients and get them to post a review on Google for you. More on this later in the book.

Main navigation

Your site's main navigation bar will be one of the most integral aspects of its success as it is one of the first things a visitor views and interacts with on your website. Ensure that it's clear and concise.

You should organize the navigation in a top-down, logical way. A 'Practice Areas' or 'Services' tab must drop down to a menu displaying organized columns or pages of your legal expertise.

Any type of 'Our Firm' or 'About Us' tab can break into a few sections that perhaps state your firm's mission or stipulate the history of the firm. But remember people hire attorneys and not law firms, so make sure your attorney bio is displayed on a page in this section.

Color Scheme

You'll be surprised to know how much the color scheme of a site contributes to its success. The psychology of colors illustrates what effect a particular color has on us.

- Red is a poignant color and is best used for CTA elements.
- White means fairness and equality
- Blue is typically calming.

If you want your site to convey auras of professionalism, try to avoid vibrant, bold colors in favor of lighter schemes. Whites, light golds, tans, light blues, and charcoals/blacks and are optimal choices.

2. Produce above-the-fold content

With a law firm site, you shouldn't get too obtuse or fancy with presenting your content. People come to your website for help with their legal predicaments, and they're probably anxious and hoping they can trust you for help.

Try to reward their effort of visiting your website by making it clear that you're there for them. To do this, present your best content above the fold. Do not make visitors dig around to find the information they require for e.g., your service page.

Depending on how your site homepage is organized, provide some links to service pages, a contact form, or even reviews to encourage trust. Sticky content like videos, surveys, forms, etc., is also a good idea.

It is an absolute necessity of well-made site architecture to present crucial information above the fold.

3. Create an effective URL structure

It's vital to get this right because you're aiming to tell search engines and human users alike what your pages are about via the URL structure of your site.

The common suggestion for generating URLs is to eliminate excess words and incorporate a few keywords. Additionally, ensure that your URLs show visitors what can be found on that page.

How Much Should Your Law Firm Spend on a Website?

The Value and Cost for a Website Redesign for Lawyers

Recognizing that your website needs an overhaul is certainly the first step towards enhancing your existing web presence. Given that your website is the most critical marketing tool that you have and given that it works around the clock for you as your online business card, your website needs to be tailored for your end readers. It needs to load quickly and be comprehensive, well-written, and properly designed.

The wrong design can lead a customer to click off quickly and to avoid taking your business seriously. However, the prospect of a website's redesign cost can be overwhelming. The cost of a website redesign can run the gamut from a few hundred dollars if you try to handle it on your own to much more for a custom built and advanced website.

There's also a cost associated with not redesigning, too. If your site is unappealing or non-functional, you could be losing clients consistently. Fixing those leaks is one of the primary reasons that law firms will consider a website redesign.

The Range of Website Redesign Costs: What You Can Expect

Perhaps you are reading this and you have a website, but it's a bit dated looking.

One of the biggest challenges for law firms in this arena is that they have no idea what they should pay for a website. Also, law firms and attorneys struggle with what they should expect to get out of it anyway.

Redesigning on Your Own

We covered this earlier, but in case you skimmed: trying to manage your own website redesign can be a big mistake. It is certainly the cheapest option but there is hassle as well as time required in the investment. Performance functionality and ease of use will vary widely but it is important to think about your end user.

Redesigning with a Freelancer

Another option for your website redesign is to hire a freelancer for this specific task. A good designer can charge anywhere from $2,000 all the way up to $15,000 or more, depending on the individual project details and the experience of the freelancer. The freelancer will work one on one with you in the best case scenario to identify your ideas, generate several different markup designs and then build from the one that you prefer the most. The downside of working with a freelancer, however, is that it can be a hit or miss experience.

If the freelancer is handling everything within the project on their own, the project could take longer and they might not have much insight as far as the marketing engine of your website beyond the design knowledge. This is why more and more attorneys are recognizing the benefits of hiring an agency for a website redesign. If you are going to work with a freelancer on your own, at least make sure they have designed a law firm website.

Hiring an Agency to Help with Redesign

The ideal situation is hiring a design agency directly who has experience in working with attorneys and law firms to handle your comprehensive website redesign. For your money, you will get a tremendous amount of value. A basic website redesign can cost anywhere from $15,000 to $20,000 although more complicated websites will cost as much as $40,000. However, the output that you get will be a kind of website that can compete with an increasingly crowded market for law firms. What makes an agency different from the vast majority of individual freelancers is the overall strategy that goes into building an effective and powerful lead generation regime.

Agencies will not only have extensive experience in the field but they tend to have more resources at their disposal as it relates to a holistic marketing strategy such as advanced tools, landing pages, content creation and all areas of design. Content is something that should always be infused into your website redesign process.

The most beneficial approach for your law firm is a content first design. The primary purpose of your website should be to connect with your audience as well as to persuade them to buy what you're offering; your services.

Your content is where the real rubber meets the road in terms of value. It is important not only for connecting with your audience but also for the purpose of search engine optimization. This is why you want to discuss content first, whether you are trying to handle this on your own, working with a freelancer or working with an agency.

An agency will usually include content as part of their redesign, making it yet another reason why law firms are increasingly turning to this option. Experienced <u>content marketers</u> on the agency's team will help guide the messaging and the content to ensure that you have a website that works for you and speaks in your tone.

Websites today are more advanced than ever and the digital landscape is evolving very quickly. If it's been some time since you've had the opportunity to revise your website, now is the appropriate chance to consider putting your website's cost into perspective.

Why Your Redesign Choice Matters

The right website can go a long way towards not just drawing clients to your site via search engine marketing and other techniques but also keeping them there and convincing them of your credibility in the field so that they contact you. Inbound marketing is one of the most critical components for law firms today and a great website can do a lot of marketing day in and day out for you. Therefore, your website needs to be the calling card that presents your law firm effectively.

Part 3:

SEO

SEO for Law Firms

Search Engine Optimization (SEO) is vital to the success of your law firm. Not just law firms, but all businesses! Now, you may be scoffing at the fact that perhaps you haven't needed SEO to get you to where you are now, so do you *really* need SEO? The answer is a resounding YES! You did not come all this way just to be seen as a mediocre attorney, did you? SEO can take you to new levels and put you ahead of your competition if done correctly. (Notice I said *if done correctly.*)

But, before we dive in any further here, I want to warn you. The SEO industry preys heavily upon attorneys and law firms of all sizes and is seeded with bad actors. These bad actors can be hard to spot but they leave trails to follow like a rat does.

1. Run from anyone who says they get you #1 on a bunch of keywords in X period of time. Do not give anyone who uses these words any of your money

2. Do not do business with anyone with too good to be true results or claims of overnight instant ranking success.

3. If it sounds too good to be true, trust that it IS!

Who should you look for to hire? Someone that asks a lot of questions about your site and what your expectations are. Someone who explains their process fully, professes to have no secret sauce, no magic pills and can offer your references. Call these references. Use your lawyer skills to detect fake references...and read online reviews. But most important, they should be able to speak to every point in this chapter with confidence and understanding.

We'll take a look over the next few chapters at the items you need to position your law firm for success with SEO, but to get us started, let's cover some basics.

What is Search Engine Optimization (SEO)?

SEO is the practice of increasing the quantity AND quality of traffic to your website through organic search engine rankings. The higher you rank on search engines, the more clicks your website will get and the more quality leads you'll get. Organic simply means "unpaid" as in you are not paying to have your website ranked in a top position (such as with Google Ads), it appears there because the "search engine gods" have deemed your website worthy.

It can be broken down into three parts:

1. On-Site SEO - Consists of items such as your meta tags, heading tags, alt-text, meta descriptions, canonicalization, robots.txt file, keyword optimization, etc. These are all things that are done **_on your website_** to improve your website's SEO.

2. Off-Site SEO - This consists of your off-site (meaning *not* on your website) that can help you improve your SEO. Backlinks, for instance.

3. Local SEO - These are your directory listings on various websites that all contain your correct NAP (Name, Address, Phone number) as well as a link (though not in all cases) to your website.

We'll explore those a bit more in depth over the next few chapters.

How Do I Get My Law Firm's Website to Rank Higher?

There are approximately 200 factors that go into how well your website will rank on Google and other search engines. Ultimately, search engines will rank you based on three elements: 1) Domain, 2) Trust and 3) Authority. They measure these three items in a number of ways. How long are people staying on your website? Are you providing relevant and valuable content? How many inbound and outbound links do you have and are they from authoritative sites? As with everything, a balance must be maintained between the three elements. If your website is optimized for SEO but you don't have any backlinks, you may not rank as well as you'd hope. This is when hiring a company well-versed in SEO for law firms, such as Precision Legal Marketing, can help push you to that coveted number one spot on Google and other search engines.

False Assumptions

Many law firms think that having a Google listing and a basic website is enough. For those that are happy to remain stagnant, maybe it is. For those that are a bit more ambitious, embracing technology and SEO practices can take your law firm to the next level.

Put yourself in the shoes of your client. Your spouse just told you that they want a divorce and you need a lawyer. What do you do? Of course, there's always word of mouth referrals, which are gold, but chances are you turn to Google or another search engine to query something like "divorce lawyer near me". First of all, you're not alone in that – the volume of people using those keywords or variations of them are astounding! Now, chances of you going past the first page are slim, but if you do keep going, you're not as likely to make it past page three or four. Those divorce lawyers who have optimized their website with the right keywords AND optimized so that search engine bots understand how to categorize the website, those are the ones that are showing up on the first page. They may be your competitor and have horrible reviews, but they know how to leverage SEO and it's keeping them in business. Are you following so far?

We can't stress the importance of keyword optimization for each and every page enough. If you're doing something, it should be done well, and it should be done with a purpose. Otherwise, what's the point of doing it? Or paying for it?

The disclaimer here is that *keyword optimization alone is not enough to rank*. You cannot just have the right keywords on your website and expect that to be enough to put your website in a top spot on Google. Many overlook (mostly because they don't understand) the need to fully optimize their website with Header-Tags (H-Tags) and Alt-Text. Keywords, Header Tags and Alt-Text are all ways that Google learns how to appropriately categorize your website. Google has search engine bots that periodically trawl your website to determine where your website should be ranking. Confusing it can not only cause you to rank poorly but can also penalize you.

Tracking Your SEO Results

This is probably the least understood and most overlooked SEO related topic we could write about. No, Googling yourself is **NOT** the answer and is not real rank results. In fact, it's best practice not to do so. If you are buying marketing services from FindLaw, Scorpion, Martindale-Nolo or one of the many other "in the box" legal marketing firms, most of what they will track is your top 5 or 10 keywords. That's never ever enough. You can read our thoughts as to why FindLaw is a poor choice for you law firm marketing here.

There are a handful of mostly useless tracking tools out there for the DIYers out there, though you will be tempted to buy paid access to them. If you are embarking on the adventure of SEO for your law firm yourself, we recommend starting with local SEO and using Bright Local as your tool of choice. It's focus is on and around your firm's address (which is how you should initially think of SEO anyway) and will let you enter target keywords you want to rank for. There is an easy to interpolate dashboard that will show you where you currently rank for the keyword you enter.

In our opinion, virtually none of the available higher end SEO tracking tools are really intuitive enough for the average user to really make sense out of, let alone exploit their full potential. However, another basic tool we do like is SpyFu, which is useful for building out PPC campaigns as well as taking a look at basic SEO data. But its flaws align with others in that your competition can mask its own results via these tools, rendering them useless. So how do you track your SEO ranking? Partner with a marketing agency that not only uses industry standard commercial grade SEO tools but understands how to apply them to the business of law.

As an example, we use a handful of tools that cost thousands a month to maintain and can provide clients with a top-drawer **daily** keyword ranking. We also summarize this ranking into weekly and monthly data points. Looking at daily ranking may seem like overkill, but with search algorithm updates on almost a bi-weekly basis, it's important to know where the curve is, and to stay ahead of it. As a consequence, we are able to actually show you what keywords you rank for, and what keywords have actual search traffic. Not a top 5 or top 10 list.

On-Site SEO

We covered SEO as a quick overview in the last chapter. To recap, on-site SEO is the search engine optimization conducted *on* your website/webpage.

On-site SEO consists of:

- Heading tags
- Keywords
- Links
- Alt-Text
- And more!

As a whole, SEO is a very big beasty and can often be hard to master without the help of an agency or SEO consultant - particularly for law firms where the competition is steep. This chapter is not meant to make you an expert, but to give you just enough knowledge to be dangerous - or at least be able to do some of the minor tasks yourself if you so choose. Another perk to learning this? It will help you spot those fraudulent marketers trying to scam you that I mentioned earlier.

Let's dive in and kick this party off with *heading tags…*

What are Heading Tags and How to Use Them

In this chapter, we will be discussing a subtle and small SEO hack that can significantly improve the performance of your law firm's website or blog post content. We are referring to *Heading Tags (H-Tags)*.

Some people might be more acquainted with these than others, particularly those who have built their own websites on any of the many web page builder applications or in WordPress; regardless of realizing their SEO value or not. However, for everyone else who is left wondering just what a Heading Tag is and why it's so important, we'll take a closer look at it as we go along.

We use heading tags in everything we publish online. In fact, you will witness more of them as you continue through this chapter, so try to spot them. Follow this guide to learn what heading tags are and how to use them to improve your content effectively.

What Are Heading Tags?

Before we move further, let's make sure that we are all on the same page. Up until now, we have used two heading tags in the guide:

- H1 for the main title at the top of the page (*A Simple Guide to Heading Tags and How to Use Them Effectively*)
- H2 for this subsection (*What Are Heading Tags?*)

And as we move further down the guide, there will be

several more used as well, so be on the lookout!

By definition, heading tags are HTML (hypertext markup language) tags that denote headers on a blog post or website. To make it even simpler to understand, tags are codes that inform a web browser how the website or blog content should be displayed on the page. They're particularly valuable in that they help the search engines, like Google, index your website. If your Heading Tags aren't used appropriately, the search engines may get confused and downrank your website as a result.

How to Use Heading Tags Effectively?

There are six kinds of heading tags i.e., from H1 to H6. Each tag is ranked from highest to lowest based on their significance and is distinctly illustrated by their font size.

H1 Tag

The H1 tag will normally be the title of the blog post or the web page, and although it is best practice to use one H1 tag per post, there should not be any negative SEO impact in case you decide to use them more than once. Marketers are probably cringing at that last statement, but this along with plenty of other myths are continuously changing or dispelled. However, that information was taken directly from Google, the search engine god that they are. Please note again that using H1 only once per page is *strongly encouraged* and should be your best practice target when possible.

Ensure that you include primary keywords that you're trying to rank for in this tag to allow search engines to understand what keywords you want the page/content to rank for.

H2 Tag

H2 tags are generally used as primary sub-headings and considered to be trivial on-page ranking factors. Therefore, we advise using them to incorporate a few synonyms of your primary keyword whenever appropriate.

This makes sense when Google analyzes a post or page heading to understand what it is about, hence including keywords in the H2 tags can allow search engines to comprehend that the content is about those keywords. Again, if the search engines can't figure out the context of the page, they won't be able to index the page appropriately and may downrank it as a result. Do not try to over optimize your law firm's webpage with H2 tags for the sake of optimizing, but it is appropriate to mix in keywords you are trying to rank for into the H tags text when natural.

H3 to H6 Tags

The remaining tags followed by the H2 tag must be used to represent the rest of the sub-heading hierarchy within a specific page or blog post.

The most crucial thing is that each heading or sub-heading must clearly define the content section it begins and logically structures the page or post.

Here is an excellent example of a logically structured post may look like:

- H1: Questions to Ask Your New York Divorce Lawyer
  - H2: When to Hire a New York Divorce Lawyer
    - H3: High-Net Worth Divorce
    - H3: Contested Divorce
    - H3: When Kids are Involved
  - H2: Pertinent Questions to Ask

- H3: Will COVID-19 Impact the Timeline of My Divorce?
- H3: How Do I Request a Modification

Pro Tip: Always structure your headings well and use primary keywords in them.

When to Use Heading Tags?

Whether you are working on a blog post or website pages, make sure to include heading tags on each page! Using them effectively will provide a hierarchical structure to your content and help readers navigate the post quickly.

It is vital to ensure that structure is not disrupted, and tags are not missed out. Failure to do so will confuse Google and make the content unstructured. Generally, H1-H4 tags are used majorly for web pages and blog posts, whereas H5 and H6 are used for very long and in-depth pieces of writing.

Why Use Headings Tags?

There are a number of reasons why your law firm's website and all of the content on it should use heading tags, including:

1. Boost SEO
2. Improve Accessibility
3. Provide Structure

Boost SEO

While Heading Tags may not directly impact your SEO, it can indirectly impact it in a number of ways when employed correctly and effectively. It creates content of a higher quality that is easier to read and a better text is favorable for users, and thus better for your SEO. The search engines prefer content that they are able to understand and classify but also, they prefer content that provides optimal user experiences.

If visitors do not easily find what they are looking for, they may leave your webpage and turn to your competition's website to answer their queries. This is why the structure and headings used in your content would impact your SEO.

Improve Accessibility

Heading structure is vital for accessibility, especially for visitors who cannot easily read via a screen. As heading tags are in HTML, a person reading from a screen can easily view and understand the article structure and content.

By listening or reading the headings on a post, visually challenged people can decide whether they want to read more about the content or not. As an attorney, I'm sure you can see the added value to this. Moreover, screen readers provide shortcuts to jump from one heading to another to provide navigation to readers.

And let's not forget that what's good for accessibility is also favorable for SEO!

Provide Structure

Heading tags allow readers to navigate through your blog post or website effortlessly, providing an optimal user experience. Therefore, it is vital to indicate what a paragraph or section is about, or visitors (and search engine bots) would not know what to expect.

Readers generally like to quickly skim through content, to decide which section of the content they are going to read. Adding h-tags drastically helps them do that as the skimming process becomes significantly more accessible for readers when it contains headings.

Now that we've covered heading tags, you may want to take a short break before continuing on. There's a lot to take in in this chapter. Go on, we'll wait for you right here.

A Law Firm's Guide to Keyword Research

Keyword research is both an art and a science. It is an SEO task that involves conducting research to find out what keywords and phrases people are using to query the search engines. Understanding what keywords people are using to find businesses in your industry can help you rank higher in the search engines. Keyword research provides marketers a better understanding of how low or high the demand is for specific keywords and how tough it will be to compete for those words in the *organic* search results while offering some direction to the optimization efforts.

There are two ways to rank on the search engines: organically and through paid advertising. When querying Google for a topic such as "keyword research" like in the image below, you'll notice that the very first result you'll see the word "Ad" before the URL. That means that to get that top spot on your search results, an advertiser paid Google Ads to have it displayed. Sometimes, there will be more than one "Ad" result. Those top results *after* the paid advertisements, are *organic* results. Organic means that the search engine (Google in this case) has determined that it is the closest possible match to your query. It's important to note that keywords are not enough to rank on the search engines, but without it your ranking efforts would be futile. If your results are not relevant to what people are querying, you'll not rank well.

Many individuals do not move past the first page of search results and those that do, they do not generally go past the third page. Those listed in the top results have an increased amount of traffic to their website, meaning quite a bit more organic exposure to a wider audience.

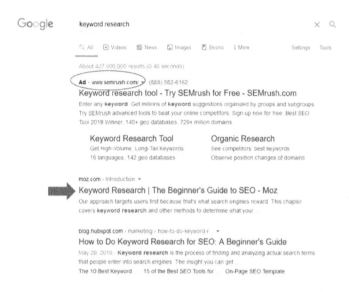

Keyword research is about validating how many searches a specific keyword has. Still, it also allows the exploration of many different ways individuals use language to search for a topic or idea. Thus, keyword researching is not just a crucial part of SEO but also a vital element of content marketing.

It can help marketers find ideas for their next article or blog post, learn about their target audience's needs, and keep up with the lingo of the always-evolving digital landscape. Ultimately, looking for keywords that people mostly use on search engines can help to create targeted content to drive the right traffic to your website and optimize the conversion rate.

The Value and Importance of Keyword Research

Although using keywords that exactly match an individual's search is no longer the most critical ranking factor, according to an SEO professional. But that does not mean that keyword research is an outdated and incompetent process.

Keyword research tells marketers what things or topics people care about and how trendy they actually are among their target audience. By researching keywords that receive a high volume of searches, marketers can identify and sort their content into topics that they want to build content on.

If you're new to keyword research and are wondering how to determine the value of your keyword; several tools can help you solve this concern and allow you to make great additions to your keyword research arsenal:

Google Keyword Planner

Google's AdWords Keyword Planner has been one of the most common starting points for SEO keyword research. Nonetheless, Keyword Planner limits search volume data by amalgamating keywords together into huge search volume range buckets.

Google Trends

Google's keyword trend is an excellent tool for discovering seasonal keyword fluctuations. For example, ''delicious thanksgiving recipes will peak in the weeks before

Thanksgiving.

Moz Keyword Explorer
Moz's keyword explorer is great for finding keywords that generate a significant amount of traffic, and what makes it more unique is that it's smart! It gives you outside of the box suggestions that you probably won't find anywhere else.

These are a few of the many tools that can help you determine and achieve high-value keywords to rank on search engines.

Surfer's Keyword Surfer
Not as well-known as the others, Keyword Surfer is a Chrome extension that you can install on your Chrome browser. When querying Google, the extension shows you an approximate number of search results and how much it might *cost per click* if running an advertisement with Google Ads for those keywords. In addition to that, it also shows you some other suggested keywords and best of all, a correlation chart showing you things like how many words the article containing those keywords in the top results of the search engine have, how much traffic those pages get, and how many keywords. Take a look at the following image:

If you're new to keyword research and don't want to pay someone, this tool is a must. You type in the keywords you're targeting, and it tells you what keywords your blog should have, how many times each keyword should be used, how many words it should have, and more. After you've published your content (and it's been indexed by Google) you can go back into Surfer to see how your content ranks, what your competitors for the coveted top spots are doing, and best of all, tips on how to get your content to rank higher (i.e. more of X keywords, increase of word count, backlinks, etc.).

Here's the link to check it out: https://surferseo.com

The Keyword Surfer extension is not meant to be an end all, be all for keyword research, but rather to provide a quick snapshot overview - for free.

Benefits of Keyword Research for SEO and Law Firms

People demand ease and convenience in all aspects of their lives, especially when it comes to online research. Several research shows that seventy-five percent of online users do not even scroll past the first page of search results. If your potential clients are not scrolling past the first page and you're not ranking there, your law firm isn't receiving as much traffic to your site (and ultimately clients!) as you potentially could (with some SEO swack ;-))

Several people believe that researching keywords is just a tool for SEO, but law firms can avail numerous benefits through this approach. New or small firms do not generally have a considerable amount of money lying around to spend on marketing endeavors like big, well-established law firms.

Therefore, using keyword research can help law firms to rank on search engines, but it is also a very inexpensive means to achieve marketing goals. Few of the many benefits of keyword research for small businesses and SEO are:

Audience Engagement

By developing relevant and high-quality content, businesses can ensure that their audience is engaged with the content and ultimately result in higher ranks on search engines. Audience engagement ensures that visitors keep coming back to your webpage for future reference, resulting in more views and prospects.

Quality Traffic and Conversions

Creating relevant and meaningful content allows businesses to attract the right kind of traffic to their webpages and increase the possibility of conversions. This factor is crucial for new or small startups to attract more audience to their brands.

Save Time

Using the correct keywords will allow businesses to save a considerable amount of time and effort. Developing content with the right keywords will not only ensure visibility but will also help to attract new customers. The lack of keyword research can make your content get lost in a sea full of other results, which is only a waste of time and effort.

How to Conduct Keyword Research?

Step 1: Make a list

The first step of this process is to come up with a list of relevant and essential topics related to your business and then use those topics to come up with a few specific keywords further in the process.

The best thing you can do is to put yourself in the shoes of your target audience and think about what topics they would be interested in searching about. This is not your final topic list but rather a big dump of possible key phrases that will ultimately be cropped to a manageable group.

Step 2: Brainstorm

Brainstorming is an integral part of this process and a great way to develop brilliant ideas for keyword research. Ask yourself similar questions during this step:

- What questions do clients ask?
- How do they talk about their problems?

- What were they searching for when they bumped into you?
- Which of your practice areas is most profitable?

The more questions you ask yourself, the better will be the final results.

Step 3: Turn to Forums and Boards

Almost every company has active forums and bulletin boards that folks turn to in search of conversation and information. It is amazing what marketers can find in these places. Such platforms are an excellent place to spot emerging trends and recurring themes.

Simply search for a 'key term + board' or 'key term + forum,' and you will most likely find something related to your business. Moreover, you can head to Wikipedia, search a few key terms, and pay special attention to the table of contents of the search result to find terms you would never have considered otherwise.

If you're looking at a specific forum, board or other web-site you search for the specific keyword and website using this in Google "site: keyword or phrase + board/forum/ website name".

Google's "site:" is an advanced search operator that allows you to see the URLs they have indexed for your **website**. Substituting your own domain for example.com, of course. May 22, 2008

searchengineland.com › what-you-can-learn-from-goo... ▾
What You Can Learn From Google's "Site" Operator
🔎 13,963,611 ☐ 1,604 🔍 0

⬤ About Featured Snippets   ▦ Feedback

For example, let's say we're looking for something relating

to the latest Facebook algorithm update. Our query and results might look something like this:

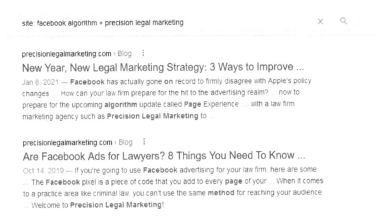

Step 4: Auto-Suggest and Related Terms

The next step is to take a few of the terms to Google and enter them into the search box. Once you begin typing, you may observe that Google starts auto-suggesting terms related to what you are entering. This is a reliable signal by Google that those terms are popular terms related to what you're searching for. Use these suggestions to expand your list and go through the related searches found on the bottom of the page to get good ideas.

For example, if we were to scroll to the bottom of our query of Google for "keyword research" these terms appear at the bottom. Those are great to help you in terms of keyword research.

Searches related to keyword research

keyword research **tools**	keyword research **meaning**
keyword research **for youtube**	keyword research **tips**
google keyword research	keyword research **process**
how to do keyword research	keyword research **methodology**

Step 5: Check for Head Terms and Long-Tail Keywords

Head terms are usually shorter and more generic, and long-tail keywords are longer keyword phrases containing three or more words. The next step is to ensure that you have a mix of both long-tail terms and head terms as it will provide you a keyword strategy that is well-adjusted for short-term and long-term goals.

Those head terms are popular search terms with high amounts of search volume. This means that the competition will be steep to rank for that keyword or phrase, both organically and paid advertising. For businesses just starting out or those that are smaller and/or working with a limited budget, targeting long-tail keywords can help you rank higher, faster without having to spend ridiculous amounts of money to get there.

Consider this. If we were to search for the term "wealth manager" we're likely to see some pretty big names in the coveted top results. If we were to convert that into a long tail keyword such as "wealth manager in Annapolis, MD" we see the competition is a bit more on par with that of a small to mid-sized business.

Indeed, there are a couple of creative approaches to

achieving a top spot on the search engines and driving more traffic to your website organically, outside of targeting those harder keywords. As a business, you're providing a solution to a problem. As a wealth manager, some of the things you may do is retirement planning, creating a custom financial plan, investment strategies, etc. Tailoring some of your keywords around specifically what you do versus your industry as a whole can be really valuable.

Some of those keywords may in fact be a question in itself. Have you ever queried the search engines with a specific question? You're not alone. We queried for "what is a long tail keyword" and in the image below you can see the answer to our question is found in a *featured snippet*, but also there are more results in the "people also search for". Take a look.

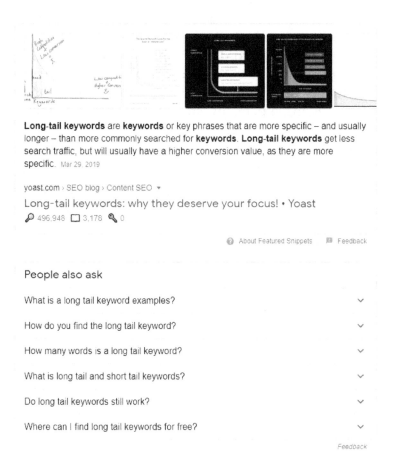

Long-tail keywords are **keywords** or key phrases that are more specific – and usually longer – than more commonly searched for **keywords**. **Long-tail keywords** get less search traffic, but will usually have a higher conversion value, as they are more specific. Mar 29, 2019

yoast.com › SEO blog › Content SEO ▾

Long-tail keywords: why they deserve your focus! • Yoast

🔎 496,948 ☐ 3,178 🔦 0

⊘ About Featured Snippets   ⊞ Feedback

People also ask

What is a long tail keyword examples?   ⌄

How do you find the long tail keyword?   ⌄

How many words is a long tail keyword?   ⌄

What is long tail and short tail keywords?   ⌄

Do long tail keywords still work?   ⌄

Where can I find long tail keywords for free?   ⌄

Feedback

Step 6: See How Competitors Rank for These Terms

Just because a keyword or keyword phrase is essential to your competitor, does not mean it must be vital for you. Nevertheless, knowing which keywords your competitor is trying to rank for is an excellent way to reevaluate your list of words.

If the competitor is ranking for a particular keyword that

is present on your list, it makes sense to improve your ranking for those terms and think about the avoided terms as an excellent opportunity to own market share on essential terms.

When conducting competitor research, it's important to have a clear understanding of who your competitors are. This doesn't necessarily mean the exact company names of all your competitors, but rather a big corporation isn't going to be a competitor of a small business, even if they are in the same industry. The fact is they have a much larger budget than a small business and likely have access to resources that a small business may not. When determining who your direct competitors are, some things you'll want to consider is this:

- Traffic to website
- Size of business (the bigger the business, the higher the budget)
- Locale (if your business is local and not national)

There are several tools out there that can help you determine what keywords your competitor is ranking for such as Moz, SEMrush and SpyFu to name a few. You're not doing anything shady by checking out the competition. In fact, your competitors are likely doing the same exact thing.

You could even work backwards if there's perhaps a keyword or phrase you're looking to rank for. Try querying the search engines for that keyword to see who ranks in the top spots for it and conduct your competitor research on those companies. If you're looking at competitors who are outside of your budget (i.e. larger companies/corporations), it's safe to say you may not see a high Return on Investment or be able to rank high for those keywords with a limited budget.

Step 7: Use Google AdWords Keyword Planner to Crop Keyword List

Once you have attained the right mix of keywords, the next step is to narrow down the list with more quantitative data. There are several tools available for this task, but Google AdWords Keyword Planner is an excellent choice for starting up. In order to get to Google's Keyword Planner, you'll need to sign up for a Google AdWords account. You do not need to pay for any advertisements to use the keyword planner.

Use any tool of your preference to highlight any words on your list with very high or low search volume. Use terms that provide you with the best balance to achieve your goals. Remember that the goal is to find keywords that you'll actually have a chance at ranking for and that your potential customers are actually using to query the search engines for. You're looking for the monthly search volume (i.e. how many people are searching for that keyword) and the metric showing how difficult it is to rank for that keyword or phrase.

Using Keywords to Rank Higher

You've got your list of keywords. Now what? Now it's time to generate some content and get those keywords on your website. You want to make sure that your main web copy (main pages and subpages such as the homepage, about, services, etc.) have the appropriate keywords interspersed throughout your content. You want to use no more than one to two keywords or phrases per page and each term should be on the page you're trying to rank for that keyword at least three times. This signals to the search engines that the keywords are important. However, be careful not to over optimize as it could make your website show as spam to the search engines, which could downrank your website.

Another item Google and the other search engines will take into account is if the keywords appear naturally. Google is all about providing an optimal user experience. So, if you're just randomly stuffing keywords in your page for the sake of having them on there, Google isn't going to place much value on that page and may in fact penalize you for it. Obviously, that is counterintuitive to reaching your goals so ensure your keywords fit into a sentence and paragraph naturally.

An example of *natural* keyword placement is this:

A new law was recently enacted in Virginia banning the use of handheld devices while operating a motor vehicle. If you're facing reckless driving charges as a result of this new law, you'll want to seek legal representation from an experienced criminal defense attorney.

Can you spot our key phrase? If you guessed "criminal defense attorney" you'd be right. See how the wording just fits in with the content? That's what is meant by the term *natural*.

Complimenting Your Keyword Efforts

Something you'll want to keep in mind is that it can take 4 to 6 months before you really notice any improvements in rankings and that keywords alone are not enough to get you to the top spot. There are about 200 different factors that Google and their bots take into account when determining how your website and page should rank. One thing you'll want to work on in addition to your keywords is increasing your Domain Authority.

Domain Authority - a term created by Moz - predicts how well a website will rank in a given search using an arbitrary score. It is NOT a percentage. The score is calculated by a number of factors including backlinks and keywords to name a few. Some people take the DA score as the end all, be all. While it is a very useful tool, it is really meant to be used as a guideline, an approximation if you will. The ideal DA range varies by industry, so don't get too hung up on the score. Newer websites and those who have rebranded may find they have a low DA, this is normal. Websites that have been around for a little while, have quality links back to their website and are ranking for some keywords should be looking for a score upwards of at least 15. Think of this as a number scoring your site to your competitors in a field like geography and industry. Though as previously mentioned, it is arbitrary.

Moz has a great (and free) tool that you can use to learn more about your website's DA and that of your competitors. There are actually several free tools that they offer in addition to their paid offerings. The link explorer tool is the one you'll want to use to check out DA. This will also show you your backlinks, inbound links and ranking keywords.

Keyword Planning for Success

Armed with knowledge and a list of tools, you can now go forth and conquer your content. I know it's been mentioned a few times already, but if you're really looking to boost your search engine ranking, you'll need to spend time on other aspects of SEO. And remember, it can take *at least* four to six months before you start noticing any ranking improvements.

Dem Links, Yo

An essential piece to the SEO puzzle is links. An effective SEO strategy employs link building methods to help drive your company up in search engine rankings. Links are generally divided into three different categories: inbound links, internal links, and outbound links. They can be defined as follows:

Inbound links: Links from another website that points to your site.

Outbound links: Links that direct you to another website.

Internal links: Links used for navigating a website or blog post by linking one page of the website to another page of the same website.

All three types of links are vital to have, but the most coveted are usually inbound links. What exactly are inbound links? And how do they benefit businesses?

What are Inbound Links?

Inlinks, inbound links or backlinks, are all the same thing. It is a simple, essential part of the internet that hyperlinks one webpage to another. Inbound is typically used by the person receiving the link and simply means links that refer back to your blog post or website.

If you've spent even a little time in the SEO industry, you'll know that SEO experts spend their entire careers specializing in gathering links. But why are they so sought-after, and how can you get them?

How Inbound Links Benefit Businesses?

In the SEO industry usually links equal profits as they drive more traffic to your website and more traffic means more potential users to convert into customers. But why is that? Read on further to learn how inbound links benefit businesses.

Benefit #1: Generate More Traffic

One of the main benefits to inbound links is that it generates more traffic to your website. Of course, more traffic means the more chances you have of converting that traffic into paying customers. Inbound links can help drive traffic to your website through two primary means: By improving SERP ranking and through referral traffic.

Improve SERP Ranking

Inbound links improve the ranking of a business website or blogpost on the search engine result pages (SERP). The higher your website is ranking for certain keywords, the more chances you will have to increase traffic on your web page. The absence of inbound links, in fact, may lower your chances to rank on the search engines (like Google) at all. Therefore, if you want to boost traffic to your website or blog post, make sure you're using inbound links in your SEO strategy.

Referral Traffic

Referral traffic comes from inbound links that direct traffic to your website. When a directory, citation, blog post, etc. links back to your website and users are clicking on that link, they are "referred" to your website by the initial website they found your link on. Hence the term referral traffic.

The volume of traffic received by a referral link depends

entirely upon the traffic received by the website or blog post in the first place. If you're looking to work on creating inbound links, you can use tools such as Moz or SEMRush to help you determine how much traffic the website in question is receiving to help determine if the link would be beneficial for you. It is crucial to ensure that you take advantage of inbound links by including information about your website/blog to the linking website. This means that you will generate traffic from your desired target audience, and this the kind of traffic that you can effectively convert into sales.

Side note: When deciding whether a link would be valuable for you, you should also take into account a website's spam score. Google does not place much value in websites that are spammy.

Benefit #2: High-Quality SEO Content

Since the inception of Google's Panda update, the quality of content on a website or blogpost matters considerably more. Those days are bygone when businesses could sprinkle poor quality content on their webpages with phrases and keywords just for the sake of doing it. But now is the era when people want content that has some worth to it. So what exactly qualifies as high-quality content?

Although there may be several other factors to contend for quality content, it is fair to accept that it embraces the following criteria:

- Creative – content should be interesting, useful and attention grabbing
- Relevant – the material should be relatable to your content
- Unique – it should be unique and not the same tired angle that your competitors are going for

Producing a plethora of content each week is futile until and unless your content is creative, relevant, and unique. To persuade other webpages to backlink to yours, it is vital that you provide *high-quality content* and ultimately escalate the number of quality backlinks to your domain.

Benefit #3: Increase Brand Awareness

Besides boosting your company's SEO strategy, backlinks or inbound links are an excellent way to build and increase brand awareness. Search engines treat quality inbound links as a sign of approval for another source. For example, if The New York Times or other authority website, backlinks to your domain, it indicates to Google that your web page is a source of relevant, legitimate, and credible information. This ensures that you climb the SERP ladder and foster brand awareness among your target audience.

By improving inbound links, businesses can show that they have done the research to find authoritative and credible pages. Moreover, social media, along with other marketing techniques, serve as a way of demonstrating authority within your industry or niche.

Benefit #4: Stay Ahead of Competition

Another key benefit provided by backlinks is to stay ahead of your competitors. Building inbound links improves your standing against other major players present in your niche industry.

For instance, if you are endorsing a service or product that is very niche, getting another player of the industry to backlink to your webpage can do wonders to put you ahead of your competitors. In a way, those links serve as an endorsement of your website.

Improving inbound strategy can significantly expose your business to a broader target audience.

How to Get Inbound Links?

Now that you know the significance of inbound links, you may be wondering how to get them. So, what is the secret behind receiving a ton of high-quality inbound links?

Although there are several tips and tricks to boost the number of links directed to your website, you can not escape the hard truth. To generate a successful link-building strategy, a significant amount of time and hard work is required. A couple of common ways to build inbound links include:

1. Develop new high-quality content that is interesting, creative, informative, and link worthy.

2. Try getting backlink references by publications, industry leaders, and other prominent figures.

3. Get the most out of existing links. Make sure the links are operational and not broken.

4. Leverage existing relationships because chances are if any publication uses your backlink, then you both might have familiar audiences.

5. Collaborate with industry thought leaders, organizations, networking groups, peers, etc. to further optimize your link building strategy.

These are only a few of the many ways you can get inbound links. Just ensure that you are producing quality content that aligns with your brand. If readers enjoy the content, chances are they will keep coming back for more.

Inbound links are a valuable component of SEO, therefore,

try to build links that entail quality and provide genuine value to your target audience. Adding links just for the sake of it can make matters worse instead of flourishing it.

Image SEO: Alt-Text

What the heck is alt-text and does image SEO *really* matter? If you're one of the ones asking that, well, you're in the right place. The short version is that *yes* image SEO matters.

If you were to query Google for something and hop over to the image results, what would you see?

If you've optimized your images effectively, you'll be able to *organically* rank well in Google's Image Search - yet another place to reach potential clients.

In the example above, we've queried "legal marketing agency" and you can see two images from Precision Legal Marketing. That's because our image SEO is on point (insert winky face).

But the value in image SEO and alt-text doesn't stop with simply ranking well (though isn't that a good enough reason to just do it??).

What is Alt-Text

Alt-Text is the written copy/text that appears if your image fails to load on a user's screen. It also benefits those users needing to use screen-reading tools to describe images to them - such as visually impaired readers. Not only that, but it also helps search engines crawl and rank your website.

Mind blown; I know.

Alt-Text is also known as "alt attributes", "alt descriptions", and occasionally (though wrongly so) "alt tags". While many CMS (Content Management System) - such as WordPress, for instance - have made it easy to quickly input alt-text without writing code, alt-text is typically written like this:

```
<img src="steveshappydance.gif" alt="Steve's
Happy Dance">
```

The key to your alt-text is to be descriptive; Explain what exactly in the image. Is it a picture of a "dog" *or* a picture of a "dog running in the park playing fetch"? Obviously, the second choice there is the optimal one.

Avoid leaving the alt-text of an image blank. Also, you'll want to avoid keyword stuffing in your alt-text as if the hounds of hell were on your heels. Keyword stuffing is where you jam loads of keywords into the alt-text of an image to try to rank for *all* of those keywords, even if the keywords are not relevant to the image. Going back to our dog running in the park playing fetch example....

"Dog, dog park, dog sitting services, kennels, dog boarding"

You should **_not_** do that. Why? Google can tell what you're doing and may ding you for it. Avoid the possibility of penalties by doing the right thing. You'll thank me for that later.

Alt-Text Best Practices

Looking to go out there and optimize your images with your newfound knowledge? Here are some best practices to help you optimize your images.

- Be descriptive and keep it in line with the image's subject and context.
- Try to stay around 125 characters or less.
- Do not start your alt-text by saying "picture of" - they know it's a picture and you're wasting characters.
- Use keywords sparingly - don't over optimize or keyword stuff.
- Each image should have a different alt-text as the images are usually not the exact same.

Understanding
Off-Site SEO

What is Off-Site SEO?

In a nutshell, off-site SEO comprises all SEO strategies undertaken outside of your website itself to raise your page's ranking on a search engine like Google.

For example, if you leave a comment or write a guest article for another blog, you are taking part in off-page website promotion. If you link back to another article or blog, you are taking an additional step of off-site SEO optimization.

Off-page SEO is often viewed to just be link building. In reality, there are many more off-site SEO tactics that you ought to use if you wish to gain a competitive advantage.

Content marketing, brand building, social media marketing, citation building, and more all play an essential role in a comprehensive SEO strategy, and it all can tie together

In short, off-site SEO covers all activities that do not involve making changes to your own site, e.g., publishing new content on it.

This helps both users and search engines perceive your website as authoritative. Moreover, they're also used as key relevance and trust factors.

Easy tip: Think of it like this:

- *Another platform or website = off-site SEO*
- *Your website = on-site SEO*

Is off-page SEO enough to rank on Google?

Without a doubt, off-site SEO is an effective tactic to improve your site's ranking. However, to rank better on Google, you would have to rely on technical and on-site SEO (refer to previous chapters). Let's explore the three core SEO approaches to clarify and understand the difference between them for improved Google rankings.

Technical SEO vs. Off-Site SEO vs. On-Site SEO

Almost all SEO strategies can be classified as one of the three types:

- On-site SEO
- Off-site SEO
- Technical SEO

Below are the key differences between these three approaches.

On-site SEO: It encompasses all tactics you use on your website to help search engines better understand and rank the content of your site. This content is everything from written to visual. From producing great content for the website, optimizing meta tags, title tags, and H tags to image optimization,internal linking, and more —all these activities fall under on-site SEO.

Off-site SEO: As explained above, it encompasses those activities taking place outside your site. Link building is generally considered to be the key off-site tactic, but it also involves tactics such as social media, content marketing, landing reviews, appearing on podcasts, building local citations, and more.

Technical SEO: It encompasses all those activities that directly impact the crawling and indexing of your website by search engines. Some people argue that it falls under on-site SEO. However, it's also broadly viewed as a discipline in its own right: structured data, site speed optimization, canonicalization, and more are part of technical SEO. This will require the use of a developer while on and off site can sometimes be considered DIY.

Importance of Off-Site SEO

Search engines like Google take into consideration several off-site factors when deciding if and where to rank web pages. Building links is one of those factors, but there are several others as well.

For that reason alone, it is quite challenging to rank solely on the merit of your content. Without off-site SEO, your site will struggle to rank for competitive search terms.

Think of off-site SEO as building your website's authority, and without it, your website would not be able to outrank those that already have superior authority. It's typically the case that content from superior authority sites ranks higher in contract to those with lower authority.

Off-site SEO is all about augmenting your site's (domain) authority, something that generally goes alongside building a brand.

There are numerous off-site SEO tactics and techniques that you ought to be using. They'll facilitate you to drive success from SEO and allow you to build your brand.

Quick Note: You will see us reference the term domain authority here. A book can be written on the term itself but all you need to know is, it's a metric used to score your website against its competition in a determined geography and business sector. It's NOT a linear metric but rather a guideline. Every website has a domain authority. You need to start by figuring out what YOURS is. I recommend heading straight to moz.com and signing up for their free domain checker now.

4 Off-Site SEO Tactics & Techniques That Work in 2021

#1: Link Building

As we just mentioned, link building must be the backbone of any off-site SEO strategy considering the influence of links in Google's algorithm. One of the key aims of off-site SEO is to build your law firm's authority. Citations are one form of a link to your site. But you want to focus on building other links as well. I know I know, you want the magic list. Start with these high domain authority sites and go from there:

1. FindLaw/Superlawyers (DA59)
   Yes I know you may hate them. Get over it. Sign up for the cheapest basic paid profile you can. The domain authority is lower than the rest, but the marketing benefits are greater.

2. HG.org (DA64)
   This is a no brainer go to site to build out a profile. They have an old school web editor you can DIY easily and pay for a basic listing with a link.

3. Lawyers.com/nolo.com (DA90)
   You might hate these guys too. The same "get over it" applies. Again, buy the cheapest paid profile you can (usually $100 a month or so) with a link to your site.

4. Justia and Cornell.edu (DA68)

   This is a great link to build because you get two for one. Call Justia and sign up for their profile and get a terrific .edu link in addition. Almost every top ranking legal website we see has this link built.

5. Avvo.com (DA71)

   We all hate this one! But build it.

Moreover, it should be able to earn quality links from authority sites. Always focus on quality over quantity. Additionally, you need to understand the link gap between your website and your competitors.

#2: Brand Building

Most people know that being listed on Google search results is rewarding for brands. Therefore, brand building activities should include not just your broader marketing and SEO tactic but also your off-site SEO approach.

#3: Content Marketing

Viewing content marketing as only an on-site SEO technique that involves content creation and publishing on your website is overly simplistic.

Take a holistic view and see how content marketing spans both off-site and on-site tactics. Publishing excellent content on your website is only one part of content marketing. You have to understand that any content you generate and publish anywhere on the web comes under content marketing. Many of the sites we listed above offer the opportunity to place written content on them and link back to your site.

The creation of engaging, valuable assets makes focusing on off-site factors easier. This usually comes from promoting the content you are producing — publishing valuable, engaging content that others want to share or link to in their content.

#4: PR

For a long time, SEO and PR were seen as two entirely different marketing disciplines. However, in recent years, these perceived differences have been blurred, causing the two to be almost merged together.

Digital PR is now used as a link-building tactic for several SEOs since it's a great way to earn authority links at a mass scale. We have our own private digital PR service that you can harness, but PR.com and others are a great tool as well.

These are just a few of the many off-site SEO tactics and techniques that can work in 2021 to help your site rank on Google.

Remember, if you want to rank your website on search engines and enhance your brand's organic search traffic and visibility, you should be looking beyond your website and linking to others in a natural way.

Understanding Local SEO

While *local SEO* hasn't come up a whole lot in the last few sections, that doesn't mean it is any less important. In fact it can be more important!

If you're working with a marketing agency or considering working with one, you'll likely hear them talk about your law firm's local SEO. What does that even mean? There are essentially three elements to <u>SEO</u>: On-site, Off-site and technical SEO. Local SEO, a form of off-site SEO, has its own benefits that can be very valuable in marketing your law firm and drawing new clients, but let's first talk about what exactly it is.

What is Local SEO for Attorneys?

Local SEO helps businesses such as law firms promote themselves online to *local* clients. Sometimes that search is done from within a proximity to your office, and sometimes the search is being done from outside the proximity of your location, but with that location in mind. As an example, a searcher may have a case in a court near your office, but be located miles away. Showing up in that search, is what we are talking about here; that's local SEO.

When someone does an internet search, particularly from a phone, the search engines gather information for local searches such as location signals, social pages, links and citations in order to show the most relevant local results to the user.

<u>Four out of five</u> consumers query search engines to discover more about local businesses, including law firms;

they are looking for legal help. Local SEO is the art of optimizing and being found for those local searches. Failure to do so could mean missing out on 80% of potential customers. For law firms whose target audience is those in the local area, optimizing for local SEO is especially important. Also, firms who want to show up in the map pack (*see screenshot below*) for their various offices need to have a local SEO strategy for each physical location, just like a national pizza chain would.

Optimizing for Local SEO

There are several ways in which your law firm should optimize its online presence for local SEO:

1. Optimize Google My Business (GMB) – GMB is the crème de la crème of local search. Do a google search right now and you will notice the map listings on the top or right of your screen! This is GMB. If your business isn't listed on GMB, you're really missing out – especially since it's free. In addition to helping you show up on local GMB listings, it also helps Google verify that your business is credible.

2. Internal Website Linking Structure – Internal linking on your website helps support website navigation, assists with information architecture and distributes page authority. Creating a seamless navigation experience with your website is important. If it's easy for consumers to use, chances are it's easy for Google to crawl and use as well.

3. Keywords – Want to show up higher in search results for your location? Ensure your website is optimized with keywords that your potential clients are using to find you. We aren't talking about keyword stuffing

a page of content, not at all. But you need to work in geography and keywords naturally into your website text. Pro-tip: link naturally out to your GMB listings here are in page content as well as blogs. Don't overdo it, just do it naturally and within context.

4. Website Meta Data Optimization – Always ensure that your on-site SEO (your website) is valid. If your header tags are skewed, Google will not know how to classify your website text and may ultimately downrank your firm's website as a result. In fact, if google doesn't find a good match for a search in your metadata, it will simply replace the meta information shown in a search. So simply looking to see what Google is actually displaying is important, as this is a basic measurement of the validity of your metadata in general.

5. Create Localized Content – In addition to ensuring that you have keywords placed throughout your main website, you should also consider implementing localized content pages for your law firm's website. These should be full length pages with woven in local keywords like criminal attorney in (cityX). Make sure this text is natural and not forced or contains duplicate content from other pages. It should be all new. This can help you improve your rankings in the search engines for localized searches. You can then use your blog to write on localized topics and link to these pages when possible. This is crucial when you're writing on relevant topics using keywords that people are actually searching for.

6. Verify your law firm's Name, Address and Phone number (NAP) – If your contact information is inac-

curate how will people find you? How will the search engines find you? In fact, Google and the other search engines may also downrank you as a result of inaccurate information. Everything has to match, which can be a pain to fix on listing websites you don't have access to like Yelp or Yellowpages.comIn that case, set up a new listing with the correct information. Usually the major sites displaying your NAP will pick up the correct address, especially when you have the majority of your listings accurately displaying. Which brings us to number seven:

7. Optimize Online Directories and Citations – This is a big one: Get your law firm listed in local online directories. Have your law firm's information pushed out to data aggregators. Ensure that through this process your information is consistent across *every* citation site. We would recommend using a site called bright-local.com to manage these listings. They even have a service that will build additional listings for a fee too. Unlike Yext, you control your listings and if you stop paying, the listings you created there will last. Do not use Yext for this purpose as they remove any built listings should you cancel their service.

Measuring Your Local SEO Performance

Once you've optimized for local SEO, how can you be sure it's working? If you're working with a marketing agency, such as <u>Precision Legal Marketing</u>, ask for them to generate a report on how well local SEO is working for you.If you're going about it on your own, here's what you can do. Install Google Analytics on your website. This is a code that will be embedded into your website and will not be visible to any website visitors. This code is used to track various metrics such as referral sources (aka how visitors are finding your website). If you're optimizing your website for local SEO keywords, you can also track keyword ranking through tools such as Moz or Rank Ranger. Brightlocal.com also has a terrific local SEO rank checker that is free or very affordable depending on what details you are looking for.

Local SEO doesn't just end there though, there's more to it than that.

Diving Deeper: The Importance of Accurate NAP's in Local SEO for Attorneys

That's a lot of acronyms and if you're not in marketing, they will not make a whole lot of sense. What is a NAP and what the heck is local SEO? Let's talk about it and why they're a crucial element to your law firm's online presence – because they are.

What is NAP?

In marketing, the acronym NAP stands for Name, Address, Phone Number and it is one of the core components of attaining high visibility in local search engines online. Having an accurate and *consistent* NAP for your business has many benefits, not the least of which is your customers being able to find you.

Local SEO and NAPs

Local SEO consists of citations. These citations are your NAP listings in directories that can help your company rank higher *locally.* The citations are what tell the search engines and other local websites where you are located, what your phone number and website are.

Citations/NAPs can contain more than just Name, Address and Phone Number – it may also include your website or various other details regarding your law firm.

Benefits of Accurate NAPs

Now that you know what NAPs are, it may be obvious as to why they need to be accurate. If your contact information is wrong and your potential customer can't find you, you've just lost business. Here's what you may not be aware of: many websites and directories scrape your information from other sites to fill their own directories and information. **So, if your law firm rebranded its name or even moved locations, it's possible you have bad contact information floating about on the web.**

Here's why it's important to ensure you've gone through and adjust those records to match your current information.

- Search Engine Ranking
- Google My Business and your NAP
- Geo-Targeted Searches
- Customers Can Find You
- Legitimacy

Search Engine Ranking

That's right, inaccurate listings can affect your search engine rankings. Here's the thing – similar to your on-site SEO, if the search engines don't have the correct information or there's a discrepancy, they'll simply downrank your website as they don't know which of the listings is accurate.

Do a search query for your law firm's name and go through the first couple of pages in Google. It will quickly become apparent if there are some issues out there that you need to correct.

Google My Business and your NAP

Google my business or GMB is the most important citation you can accurately have setup for your law firm. In fact, trat this citation as your default. Ensure everything looks as you would have it look everywhere on the internet including the fine details of your name. If you do nothing else after reading this, go to google and make sure you have your GMB listing claimed and properly filled out. If you thought passing go and collecting $200 was important in monopoly, then this will be your favorite marketing ploy of the year. As we mentioned above, many citation aggregators pull their information first from this citation. So, it is critical that it be accurate. Make sure to include your hours of business, photos (more than one), your logo and more. Basically, fill in as much information as you possibly can, upload your logo and images too.

Geo-Targeted Searches

Remember we talked about there being three aspects to SEO? Your NAP and the citations connected with it do help your overall rank on the search engines. For instance, if we were to query the search engines for "family lawyer in Virginia Beach", those citations in the various directories will help your law firm show up in the correct location. A law firm located in Maryland would not necessarily show up in the search results for "family lawyer in Virginia Beach" as they are not located out of Virginia Beach. They would have no citations in that area and no keywords on their website either. This is why SEO is so important, it literally helps to control where you show up geographically, for the right keyword searches.

Customers Can't Find You

If you have inaccurate information on your listings, your customers aren't going to be able to find you and will quickly move on to your competition. Without having good reason, many clients aren't going to dig through various results to find your correct information. So, you want to make sure that they get it right the first time.

Legitimacy

When it comes to finding new clients, ranking in the search engines, etc. you really have to prove that your website and law firm are legitimate. One way to do that is through enhancing your SEO efforts with local SEO/citations. Get your firm's name out there and listed in as many places as possible. Trust me, your competitor has already done just that for their own law firm.

Whether you're going it alone or looking to hire a partner for your marketing, here are three crucial elements you'll want to keep in mind:

1. Have a SOLID local SEO and map pack ranking. Addressing both search and Google Maps will take a more comprehensive approach to your SEO digital marketing efforts.

2. Work with a certified Google partner who puts an emphasis on local SEO so that you can combat the big boys in your city. Certified Google partners have the latest information on Google best practices that will benefit your firm.

3. Find smaller GEO's to rank in. This is often an over-looked but valuable note… to plan out and execute. For example, say you have an office in Fairfax, VA and you rank well there. But what about ranking well

in Tysons or Vienna? With mobile and geo keyword searches you have a shot at beating these big dudes to first page ranking.

How Legal Directories Can Benefit Your Law Firm and Your Seo Efforts

Legal directories came into being approximately thirty years ago as a kind of 'Yellow Pages' for law firms and attorneys. At its most elementary level, a legal directory is a searchable database of lawyers sorted by practice area, location, and other attributes.

An entry in a legal directory encompasses an attorney's firm affiliation, their contact information, and their work experience. However, today, several legal directories offer additional benefits, such as publications, ranking, and customized marketing opportunities.

Read ahead to find the answer to "how legal directories can benefit your law firm."

4 Perks of Being Listed in a Legal Directory
The following are some of the benefits of legal directories:

Greater visibility due to SEO
First and foremost, legal directories can help you get your name in front of organizations and individuals who are seeking legal help. There's no denying that more and more people are heading to the internet for research before making a purchase.

Similarly, when somebody types something like 'family lawyer in New Jersey,' usually legal directories are some of the first links that emerge due to their rich SEO. If somebody heads to one of the legal directories and begins scrolling through the list of lawyers, would you not want your name to be there?

The more legal directories you are a part of, the greater your chance of acquiring a new client.

Improved website ranking on Google

A legal directory can also help your website to rank better on search engines like Google. Most directories attach a link to your firm's website along with your listing; this is known as a backlink. When a huge, credible site backlinks to your website, it helps to boost your SEO. This means that you are not only more visible up on Google through your legal

Receive greater credibility through directory rankings

Some legal directories involve a ranking component, for e.g., only attorneys with verdicts over a particular amount are listed in the directory. Therefore, being highly categorized can offer your company the supplementary credibility that convinces a customer to select you for their legal needs. Moreover, your inclusion can be leveraged with customized videos or a digital badge for your site. This can create extra PR for your law firm.

Provides reviews and rating by previous clients

Numerous legal directories also provide an option to your previous clients to give ratings or reviews for your services. That is a great resource considering that many people nowadays are more likely to appoint an attorney after going through reviews online. Furthermore, it creates an excellent opportunity to engage previous clients and requests them to share their feedback on your directory listing, where more prospective clients will be able to see it.

4 Worthwhile Legal Directories to List In

With so much to offer, a legal directory ought to have a place in any law firm's PR plan. However, this begs the question: which legal directories should you be on? There are more than a hundred options to choose from, but here we have narrowed down to four for your ease.

#1: Justia

As one of the topmost legal directories, Justia offers a decent amount of referral traffic and covers over 5.3 million keywords. They're one of the highest-rated legal directories regarding authority, and the backlink offered passes authority. Moreover, a standard listing is entirely free! Their clients can benefit not only from enhanced local rankings by acquiring a listing on Justia but also through receiving referral traffic and leads.

#2: Avvo

Similar to Justia, Avvo is a foundational directory that every lawyer should acquire a listing on. Plus, the listing is free of cost; they have an excellent reputation and are listed on over 1.9 million keywords. However, one thing to keep in mind is that Avvo's links are 'nofollow.' Hence, authority from the links do not pass, but the citation is authoritative.

#3: FindLaw

FindLaw has obtained over 4.2 million keyword rankings and is more recognized in the legal industry as a quality directory. They also offer a substantial amount of authority. However, as a part of the Thomson Reuters network of websites, the listing on this directory does cost money.

You'll have to contact them to schedule a meeting and negotiate a listing that best suits your requirements. Nonetheless, we can't disregard the command of this citation. The links back to your site do convey authority, and the citation is of great value. Moreover, with the correct value proposition, the lead generation value can extend past the search engine optimization (SEO) value.

#4: Best Lawyers

Best Lawyers directory is a high authority site, with one hundred twenty-three thousand keyword rankings, do follow backlinks, and the best thing is that the listing is free! But there's a catch – you will have to be nominated. But this nomination can come from anywhere. Plus, if you get selected as a top lawyer, the marketing potential and value goes far beyond local law firm SEO.

Indeed, the legal directories that conduct research to qualify attorneys and law firms they list can be considered more credible than those directories where you have to pay to be listed. But that does not mean that the paid directories should be overlooked.

The SEO value and visibility that they offer can't be denied. It is best to evaluate your available resources and time to determine what mix makes best suits your law firm. If you are just beginning your SEO journey or hanging a shingle, this is the best place for you to start your marketing efforts. Sign up for the minimum amount spent but still get a valid do follow link back to your site. Then ramp up front there.

As a bonus resource, we've put together a list of 107 different websites/directories to get your law firm listed on at the back of the book.

Should My Law Firm Have A Google My Business Listing?

Google My Business is a free way to gain exposure for your law firm. It's been around for a while, and chances are you have seen these listings yourself. If you were to Google a competitor firm right now, chances are you will see their listing immediately pop up in the search engine, and you will see their location, phone number, hours, and other information they chose to list.

This is a key piece of real estate on a search result page, as these map results are on top of organic rankings on desktop, and at the top of a search on a mobile device. As an Attorney, you need to embrace Google My Business now, if you haven't already. But what if you are an associate or partner of a law firm? You may want to search yourself and your colleagues, Google has been busy trying to add you as an individual attorney to it's Google My Business listings too. If you see yourself there with a listing and want to know how to claim it, keep reading or give us a call and we can walk you through the process.

How People Actually Use Google My Business & What it Offers

With as much as you can do with Google My Business, you'll probably be shocked that it doesn't cost anything to use. There are several uses for it, including finding where you are located. But it offers so much more:

1. Check Opening Hours

Many people want to know an answer to something right away. Either they are too busy to make a phone call, or they just want the answer at their fingertips. With Google My Business, people can just type your business name and your hours will appear.

2. Convenient Directions

Let's pretend you just got off the phone with a potential new client. You gave them your address, but everyone uses GPS these days, right? They hop in the car to drive to their consultation and what do they do? Pull out their smartphone to navigate. I know I do! They can conveniently click "map" and their GPS will give them voice directions to your address. GMB is also directly connected to Google Maps and it's smartphone apps on both Apple and Android devices. It also drives results in voice search (especially important on Android devices) so it's pretty important to make sure you are there.

3. Reviews Build Trust

When searching for a lawyer, it's only natural that someone would want to ensure they are hiring the best possible option for their case. Not only can an individual access your firm's phone number and location instantly, but they can check reviews on demand. The more reviews you have, the more trustworthy your practice will be to the person searching, and to google. Studies have shown the more reviews you have on your google my business listing, the more often Google will show you in a search.

4. Drives Website Traffic

Be sure your website is up-to-date, full of rich blog content, and engaging to your audience. You are bound to receive a lot of traffic to your website just by listing your business as there is a website link right in the listing itself.

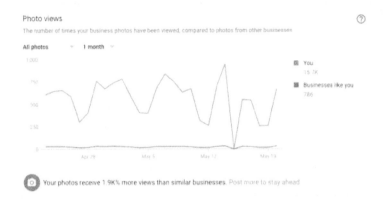

Track your photos' views to that of your competition.

5. Take Plenty of Photos and Add Them

Another way to gain trust is to add photos to your listing. Upload pictures of the outside of your office, lobby, conference room and even you at work at your desk. There is a spot for your audience to scroll through these pictures. The business can add photos, along with people who visit. Show your true personality. Have fun with your staff and post the photos. By doing this, you're giving them a good impression before they make the first phone call.

6. Popular Times to Visit

There is a spot on Google My Business that shows the popular times your office is visited the most. Most people don't have time to wait, and if they don't have an appointment they will want to see when you're not so busy. This is a great feature that will allow them to find out on their own what time they should go.

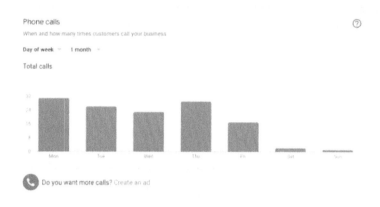

See when people are calling your firm the most. You can also sort this by time of day giving you even more powerful information.

7. Call With the "Tap" of a Button

Just about nobody uses a phone book anymore. It's all digital. When someone is looking for a lawyer and they Google it, your listing will show up. The more convenient thing is that just by tapping the "call" button, it will automatically put the phone number into their smartphone and all they have to do is push call. Our mobile driven society has conditioned us to use these embedded buttons. A pro-tip is to use call tracking numbers to track these phone calls. A useful tool when keeping a marketing agency (who uses GMB as part of their SEO strategy) honest, and looking at phone traffic increases over time.

8. Questions and Answers – Direct Interaction With Your Firm

People can easily ask a question right on your firm's business listing. Other people who have experience with your law firm can answer, or you could go on and answer. The great thing about this is that other people can view past questions in case they were also curious. They will also see others interacting with your business listing, building even more trust. Make sure you or your marketing agency is there to answer these questions as soon as possible, google is watching how long you take to get to these questions. As a registered owner of the listing, you will receive an email when someone posts a question. If you download the official GMB app, you can answer questions right from your smartphone.

Can My Law Firm Track Google My Business Results?

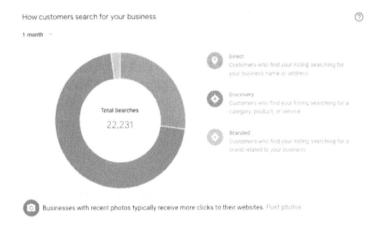

Google Insights tracks a number of important metrics. Select a longer duration of time to see how your listing performs over the long haul.

Google My Business + Tracking Tools = Measurements for Success!

Once you add your law firm to Google, there is a tool called Insights to see how your listing is performing and you can see the conversion rates. It's helpful to know which of your marketing efforts are paying off, so you know what's working. Much of this information can be sorted by dates too, so you can see how optimizing your listing has had an affect on its performance.

It's not just about tracking the leads back to your website, though. Bright Local recommends using a unique call tracking phone number to see what percentage of people are calling based on your listing alone. Google My Business can report which callers are using the "click-to-call" function but they can't report on who is physically typing the number after viewing the listing.

Importance of a Fully-Optimized Google My Business Listing For Your Law Firm

Anyone can go on and throw up their hours, address, and phone number on a Google My Business Listing. However, if you want to be truly successful with it, and you want to see those results, it's important to fully optimize the listing.

You're going to have to dig deep to do keyword research and carefully add them in naturally. Any old keywords just won't work. This is an important step that can't be missed.

Don't skip the photos, either. According to Search Engine Journal, businesses with photos receive 42 percent more requests for driving directions. Photos also lead to 35 percent more click-through rates to the business' website. Photos will have to follow the Google best practices.

Once your Google listing is up, it's important to interact with your visitors. Check for questions on a consistent basis and always follow up promptly. If someone leaves you a review – good or bad – be sure to respond professionally and politely.

Keeping Your Firm's Online Reputation Updated

It's often said that we are passing through the information age, and are now moving towards the reputation age.

This is where the court of public opinion significantly influences decisions being made on what products or services are being purchased where, including where people will obtain their legal services.

When one of your clients searches for legal services, they will often look at online reviews from other people that can be seen on such sites and apps like Google, Facebook, Yelp, etc...

These online reviews can be easily managed by responding to each reviewer and ensuring the person providing the review is satisfied with the answer provided and are willing to update their review if needed. This form of interaction allows a level of transparency that shows you and/or your firm are willing to ensure that a client/customer is satisfied.

Many times the deciding factor in getting a potential client to call you is due to a review someone left on some site or app. It could be a negative one that was handled in a positive way that impressed a potential client.

But online reputation goes far beyond just simple reviews left on websites and apps. It's about managing any data associated with your Firm that can be found online, by ensuring whatever information a potential client can see online is updated and is accurate.

Here are a few items to consider when addressing your online reputation, including simple reviews:

1. Websites

We know that websites should be seen on mobile devices and professional looking. But did you know that content on those sites need to be reviewed regularly?

Every part of a website needs to be updated, not just for SEO, but to also ensure that the content on each page is accurate. And we're not just talking about spelling and grammar.

For example, a game plane to handle content on your firm's website that is associated with a partner should be in place in case a partner leaves your Firm. You should make sure any content that highlights the former partner is updated appropriately.

2. Social Media Accounts

Beyond keeping track of reviews on such platforms as Facebook and Google+, regularly sharing appropriate content through these channels helps to showcase your firm's interests and expertise. Having some content pushed through these avenues boosts your Firm's public image.

3. Listings

Your Firm may be listed on hundreds of directories and websites. Each listing may not only include your firm's name and contact information, but also include all of your firm's partners as well.

If your office moves, if your phone numbers change, or if

a partner is added to your firm or if a partner leaves, all of these listings need to be updated.

cough *local SEO* *cough*

4. Search Engines

SEO is search engine optimization. Part of managing and improving SEO is ensuring the right website pages and content are being shown on first page results when someone looks for your services. Also, a part of this process is finding content on other websites that should be updated and/or scrubbed from search engine databases.

It's typically best to work with a Google Certified Partner to help get online information updated correctly, including the removal of content from Google search engine.

This may be required if a partner leaves a firm.

5. Revisit Reviews

As previously stated, we are moving into the reputation age. Reviews are the first thing a potential client sees, and it's the first sign of where your law firm's reputation takes place. Not taking the time to address these reviews in some fashion may show potential clients that there is a lack of care.

From responding to a review when it first gets posted to soliciting reviews from clients, you can help provide some positive light on all the efforts you and your Firm have been doing.

Keeping your law firm's online reputation in check not only ensures you are managing some basic public image issues, but also helps to reduce potential liabilities. After all, the last thing your firm wants to distribute is misinformation.

How to market on Quora, Reddit and other Q&A forums

Millions of internet users use online forums to seek advice on pressing issues. Quora is by far the most popular forum with over <u>300 million</u> monthly users. Quora answers often show up as snippets on Google search results, which means that your Quora answer can have a reach far beyond Quora users. For that reason, this article focuses on using Quora, but the tips explained here can be easily applied to other Q&A platforms.

Overall, your use of Quora should carefully balance thoughtful, helpful responses with **indirect** marketing. This is probably more of an SEO play than any meaning marketing. In other words don't expect the same type of return from this as you would say answering questions on Avvo. That said this is a less traveled road than other marketing avenues, so you may find it useful. Internet users have become quite deft at detecting online advertising, and often ignore or discount advice that is laden with marketing. Your answers on Quora should encourage users to click on your profile where your firm's information will be listed. We actually recommend avoiding mentioning the name of your law firm anywhere in your written response to a question, as this can appear too much like an advertisement and not genuine advice.

How To Build An Effective Quora Profile

A professional and credible profile is key to your success on Quora. You should include your name as it appears on your firm's website, a professional picture, and a brief description. The description can summarize your experience and education. Some users like to add more personal information about their hobbies and interests.

Your profile will also show what you do on the site. Users can see how many questions you've answered, your followers and who you follow, questions you've asked, and more. Your profile will also show a list of your recent activity.

A key part of your profile is your "credentials," which provides users with valuable information about your skills, experience, and education.

- Your **"Profile Credential"** is a short description that users see under your name when you answer questions. A well-optimized Profile Credential section will showcase your specific experience. You also will want to include your location to encourage local users to contact you if your practice area is limited to your city, region, or state. Here are a few examples:
  - Criminal defense lawyer (NY), former law professor
  - Patent lawyer, 10+ years of experience, firm partner

- Other credentials you can add include your education, employment, and location. Don't skip this step. Displaying your J.D., law firm, and the location is crucial to turning profile visitors into clients.

How To Find and Answer Questions

Use the search bar to search for legal questions related to the coronavirus. You can search broadly using terms like "coronavirus legal issues" or "coronavirus and the law," or be specific and search things like "coronavirus business interruption insurance lawsuit." When you click on a question, a list of related questions will appear to the left.

Once you find a good question to answer, you'll want to answer with some helpful information. You can't provide legal advice, but you can explain how the law might apply to the situation and what legal options might exist. You're writing to a lay audience — avoid using legalese or being overly specific.

Remember to avoid sounding like you're advertising your services. Do not mention or refer people to your firm in your answer. Focus on making your answer helpful and informative, so that users want to click on your profile, follow you, and learn more about your firm. Unless the user explicitly asks for advice on hiring a lawyer, keep your answer limited to a general explanation of how the law might apply to their situation.

Building a Good Reputation

The best way to increase exposure to your law firm on Quora is through consistent and high-quality engagement. Users can "upvote" answers that they find helpful, and answers with many upvotes are more visible, both within Quora and on search engines like Google. If a user finds your answer particularly helpful, they might choose to follow you, which means that they will receive notifications about your activity on the site. You can and should also follow other users. Quora also rewards users who provide frequent, well-rated answers with various badges and distinctions displayed on your profile, such as "Top Writer."

If you're struggling to find enough specific questions seeking advice about coronavirus and the law, try engaging more broadly. Many Quora users ask questions like, "Do people suing cruise lines have a good chance of winning their case?" Answering questions like these will help you build your reputation as a thought leader in this particular space. It is also a good idea to focus on answering questions about topics that you are particularly interested in or have experience with. Simply enter a few keywords pertinent to your practice and you will likely find many questions to answer.

Part 4:

Content Marketing

What is Content Marketing?

What is content marketing? Content marketing is exactly what it says - content used for marketing. Content marketing is a strategic approach to marketing, providing new avenues to provide *relevant and valuable* content to your current, former and potential clients. It is conducted with the intent of lead generation and building on brand awareness and brand recognition. Don't worry, we'll get to what those terms mean and why they're important in a few minutes. For those with a creative flair, content marketing can be a really fun and creative opportunity to showcase your law firm and expand your reach.

Content marketing includes (but is not limited to) graphics and other posts on social media, blog posts, articles, videos, webinars, infographics, podcasts, eBooks, templates, newsletters, etc. (Check out the end of the book - we've put together a list of 107 different types of content!) It is a piece of content used to not only build brand awareness and brand recognition, but also to generate leads for your law firm. Chances are pretty high that if you haven't created any of the aforementioned, you've definitely at least seen some of those items. If you're on social media, you've definitely been on the receiving end of some content marketing tactics. Every day, law firms are paying to have their content displayed on your news feed.

Some of those may seem pretty intimidating - I'll confess, as I sit here writing this book counting every single word,

I'm asking myself what the heck did I get myself into. If some of those seem to be a bit intimidating, there are bound to be other areas that you can excel at. If your law firm can afford it, you could even consider hiring someone to create that content for you.

In addition to driving traffic to your website and snaring leads in your sales funnel, content marketing also has another key benefit - helping to establish you as a thought leader in your practice areas. You want to be an established and respected <u>authority</u> in your practice areas? Generate some content that demonstrates your knowledge and expertise. Provide value. Your information should not be over broad but should be technical and thorough while speaking directly to your audience. When writing your content, you should not assume that your audience understands your practice areas at the level you do, and you may need to word things a little differently. Break down that technical talk in a way that is easy for all to understand.

Going forward with this knowledge can be a great stepping off point for your content marketing strategies. Why not create some graphics or blogs that break down some of the basic concepts of your practice areas? If your clients were experts in your practice areas, chances are they wouldn't be your clients - they'd be your competition.

Let's look at how it can benefit your law firm:

1. Increases visibility
2. Improves brand awareness and brand recognition
3. Develop lasting relationships
4. Creates brand loyalty and trust

5. Builds authority and credibility

6. Positions you as a thought leader in your practice areas

7. Generates traffic to your website

8. Provides value

There are those words again: brand awareness, brand recognition, lead generation... what??? We get that some of you reading this are aware of what those terms mean and so we'd encourage you to skip ahead if that's the case. Here's a quick snapshot of the terms - this book will cover brand awareness and brand recognition a bit further on in the book to help you gain a better understanding.

Brand awareness is important for all law firms, not just those who have been in the game for a while. Building brand awareness is especially important for law firms just starting out. Think of it like this, if no one knows about your law firm, there's not likely to be much traffic to your website or social profiles. Building brand awareness is about saying "Hey, I'm here! Come check me out!". Brand awareness helps people build impressions about their law firm and/or services.

When you query a search engine for something, chances are you're "Googling" it. This is a great example of brand awareness. Google is in fact a brand and not the appropriate terminology to describe what you're doing. This brand awareness associates your services with a particular action, more often than not subconsciously. In this case, Google is being associated with searching or querying for something.

Keep in mind that building brand awareness doesn't just happen overnight. It takes time and effort and goes beyond advertising for your service. In fact, brand awareness is about adding in the human element to your marketing.

Have you been on Twitter lately? Wendy's has been knocking them out of the park with their straight savagery and it is hilarious! The fast-food chain dominated social media by exchanging banter with followers and even going so far as to "troll" their competitors. This direct engagement with their followers and the ensuing spotlight to follow brought the law firm a HUGE increase in their net income. Their strategy put people back into their marketing efforts. It's not just about ramming sales pitches and pictures of tasty food (if you're in the food practice areas) down customers' throats until they unfollow you, it's about providing value and connecting with them.

So, now that we know what brand awareness is, what is brand recognition? While it can easily be confused with brand awareness, brand recognition is its own entity. To recap, brand awareness is about making people aware that you exist. Brand recognition is the extent to which people recognize your brand. Going back to fast food (can you tell it's lunch time and I'm hungry?!), when we see or think about golden arches, our minds automatically associate it with McDonald's. And the list goes on.

All right, now that we've cleared that up let's get back into talking about the benefits of content marketing.

Benefits of Content Marketing

There are many ways to gain traction for your law firm. Sitting there thinking that people will flock to your shop simply because you exist is not one of them. One of the benefits of content marketing is increased visibility. Unless you're paying for advertising or to have the content curated for you, writing blog posts, designing graphics can both be done for free. Publishing them to your social profiles is also free. With millions of daily users on social media EVERY DAY, this is your opportunity to shout from the roof and let people know that you exist. It's not just posting to social media either - your blog posts can help you rank for keywords in the search engine and help you be found easier, provided they're appropriately optimized for search engines.

While the majority of your content should focus on building and promoting your brand, in order to drive engagement, you should also create content that your followers want to interact and engage with (like, comment, share). Let's look at Star Wars Day: May the 4th be with you. Star Wars has such a huge cult following that it's easy to get swept up in it. Star Wars Day is a day that trends organically, meaning big law firms aren't paying to have it pumped up. All across social channels you'll see individuals, non-profits, influencers and law firms of all shapes and sizes jumping on the content train producing intergalactic images to delight their followers.

Your law firm's marketing strategy as a whole and your content marketing strategy in particular should be a continuous effort to build brand awareness and brand recognition. Whether you're writing a blog, posting to social media or hosting a webinar, work to build positive and lasting impressions so that when someone thinks of a service your name comes to mind. Consider this: if you've ever been injured you've likely asked for a Band-Aid. See those capital letters there? That's because Band-Aid is a brand and is not the name of the actual product. The word you're looking for here is actually bandage. Be the Band-Aid of your niche.

Develop lasting relationships. Content marketing often allows direct or indirect engagement with your current, former and potential clients. Providing consistent and valuable content can help to keep your law firm at the forefront of their mind. Your customers won't need your services every day, they won't buy an item from your shop every day. When the time comes that they are in need of the services that your law firm offers, you want your law firm's name to be the first name to come to mind (and not just for something negative).

Create brand loyalty and trust with your current, former and prospective clients. The world is your oyster! Offering content to your audience that is educational, provides solid advice or other useful resources *freely* (i.e. no strings attached, no sales pitch) can help your audience feel confident that you are an expert and you're not just trying to make a buck. Relationships built on trust are more likely to convert to a qualified lead and generally have a higher lifetime spend than average customers.

Use it as a way to help you build authority and credibility. Demonstrate your expertise by providing resources and educational materials to your audience. Again, keep in mind that not everything should have a price tag on it. Those outside of the financial sector may not understand what a bull and bear market is. Explaining those things can help your audience come to look at you as an authority on the subject which only further boosts your credibility.

Continuing along this path, establish yourself as a thought leader in your practice areas. It takes time to get there, but you have to start somewhere. All you have to do is take that first step. And then another and another. Once you've established yourself as a practice area thought leader, people will naturally turn to you to find the answers they're looking for. I know what you are thinking. I don't have any huge noteable cases, no settled law to my credit and I have never argued before SCOTUS. Hell, you might not even be licensed to practice in federal court. That is NOT what we are talking about. What we mean here is the thought leader in your local geo (first) in your practice area. This can be where quality over quality takes a seat at table. Write as much about your practice areas as you possibly can.

Yet another benefit of content marketing is the fact that your content helps drive traffic to your website, pushing those potential leads further down the sales funnel and hopefully converting to a qualified lead. *Quality* inbound content to your website helps create a larger digital footprint and increases the chances of being found in the search results.

While I'm sure there are more reasons why content marketing is beneficial, I'm going to leave off with this last one - it provides value. More than anything, your content provides value to your audience. Bearing in mind that the larger percentage of your audience will not convert to a sale, you should still continue to provide valuable content. It can be frustrating to produce content for an audience that won't convert, but for all of those that don't there will be those that do convert. So, keep trucking.

As many states across the nation declared shelter in place orders during the COVID-19 (novel coronavirus) pandemic, many law firms were forced closed after being deemed non-essential. How would these law firms pay their employees or their rent with no law firm? While many took some pretty damaging losses, others found innovative ways to generate income and remain relevant. Paint and wine places started offering virtual paint sessions and take-home kits to work on at your leisure. Restaurants began offering meal kits and curbside pickup.

These law firms turned to social media to spread the word by posting graphics and videos saying, "We're still open!" I can't tell you how many law firms I've seen advertising on Facebook through all of this. One of those law firms was a restaurant located several <u>hours</u> north of me. The restaurant wanted to let people know that they were still open and that they were offering free delivery within a five-mile radius. Needless to say, I'm well outside of this range. Do you know how much money they probably wasted on this ad?! I contacted the restaurant through Facebook Messenger to let them know they probably needed to refine their target audience and take a look at their geographic range. After thanking me, they admitted that they had accidentally targeted the ENTIRE United States!

It was because of them that I ended up creating a short guide on Facebook Advertising best practices and started offering it for free. Do you know how many small law firms across the nation are in peril after being forced shut? There will always be law firm for marketing agencies. I don't need to charge money for something that could benefit so many in a time of need.

The takeaway here is that if you're doing things right, law firm will come. There will be some who could benefit from the free value-driven content you produce that don't convert to clients. Take comfort in knowing that you're helping someone out. Just like the saying during COVID-19, we're all in it together. And the person you might help out may know someone who is looking to convert and that positive experience they had with your law firm could lead to a word of mouth referral of your services.

Designing graphics or making videos or even writing an SEO formatted blog the search engine gods will approve of may seem daunting, but there are so many resources out there to set you on the right path. And if you're still stuck after reaching the end of this book, I hope you'll reach out.

When writing content for your website such as web copy (the words on each main page of your website) or creating some awesome blogs, you'll want to ensure that they're all formatted properly and optimized for SEO success. SEO is the backbone to content marketing.

The Psychology Behind Law Firm Content Marketing

Understanding *who* you are marketing to can help you identify *how* to market to them. You need to put yourself in the shoes of your target audience and think about what would resonate best with you. What *tone* should your content have? What emotions are you trying to elicit and why? What emotions are you trying to perhaps calm? What colors will send the right message to them?

Understanding the answer to those questions can help give your content marketing strategy a boost.

What is Tone in Marketing?

The tone of your content is *how* your content is written. This should illustrate how you feel about the subject being written, guiding your target audiences' emotions, helping them understand how they should feel. Do you want them to be inspired? Informed? Entertained? Knowing what resonates best with your target audience can help you determine the appropriate tone. For instance, will you inject some humor to break up the monotonous of a topic that would normally be less than intriguing? Perhaps you'd like to inspire and motivate by injecting some inspirational quotes or examples of people/companies who have benefited from the topic.

Some examples of tone include:

- Joyful
- Inspirational

- Humorous
- Informational
- Formal/Technical
- Sad
- Optimistic
- Etc.

The tone you decide to encompass in your firm's content can help showcase your brand personality and values.

The Value of Emotion

What does your content mean to your audience? How do you get them to read your content let alone convert to a client? **You need to offer them a connection.** Emotional marketing tells your story in a way that helps your audience connect and relate with your content in a personal way. Many studies have been conducted demonstrating that consumers will more often make a purchase based on emotions over logic. They will also select an attorney this way. Logic comes more into play when we try to justify the amount of money, we either have or are about to spend.

How well does your content provide an emotional connection to your audience?

Emotional marketing is when marketers use emotion to get your target audience to take notice, remember, share and retain your law firm.

Think about how many times a day you see an advertisement online... You checkout Google - advertisements all over. You visit your favorite online retailer to see if they have any deals on - advertisements. Scroll through your social accounts - you just can't escape advertisements, and neither can anyone else. In a sea of advertising, you want yours to stand out and be memorable.

Note: There is that dirty little word in legal marketing: *advertising!* Contrary to the belief of some, as an attorney it's okay to advertise your services. Of course you may not directly solicit for business. But marketing your services or advertising them is completely legal as well as ethically. You should absolutely consult your state bars ethics and rules of advertising, as well as the American Bar Associations same information.

Now, let's compare advertisements. Let's step outside of the business of law for a moment.

Company A is featuring a baby blanket. The advertisement just has the brand name, the product and the name of the product.

Company B is also featuring a baby blanket. Their advertisement has a cute little baby running around with their baby blanket before falling asleep with the very same snuggly blanket they refused to put down all day.

Which advertisement elicits the most emotion from you? Is it the plain Jane? Or is it one that maybe makes you think about your own children or other loved ones? And how long did it take you to decide that? You have only a couple of seconds to make a good first impression and captivate your audience.

Jessica: Thinking back on my own impulsive buy and it was a nail kit that I stumbled across through a Facebook Advertisement. I got caught in their pixel, guys! With being stuck in from the quarantine, salons barely open and working long hours I started to feel like I was letting myself go a bit. There were a few days in there that I'm not even sure that I brushed my hair, let alone changed out of pajamas. So, when that ad came across my timeline, I started *feeling* like maybe I could use some self care and liked the idea of salon quality nails at home. (I have no regrets by the way) You see, the company realized that there is an increased demand for their product - salon quality nails at home for an affordable price - and they set out to create advertisements that would bring in the business. In the wake of COVID, you can bet I'm not the only one excited about the nail kit!

Steve: My impulsive buys have been many, especially on Facebook. I was also caught by the Facebook pixel, but in a different way. I had been looking to send my cookware set back to calphalon to take advantage of the lifetime warranty. Literally an hour later I was buying skillets on Facebook from Hexclad (highly recommended) while scrolling through my news feed. Hexclad's pixel had determined I was in their interest group from my earlier web and voice searching that day.

Think back to some of your own purchases and the emotions the advertisements may have invoked in you.

Let's look at how some marketing tactics employ emotional marketing into their campaigns.

Happiness

Happiness is contagious, even online. Studies have been conducted by various organizations that demonstrate that good news and positive content spreads faster on social media than any other content. If you're looking for engagement and shares, this is a sure-fire way to get them.

Happiness makes us want to share.

Sadness

Empathy leads to altruism and the motivation to act on

behalf of others. This emotion inspires people to act and help people or organizations. Why do you think you see some many advertising featuring small, starving children and animals?

Sadness makes us empathize and connect with one another.

Surprised

When surprised - whether good or bad - we tend to seek comfort from things that we're comfortable with. Surprise can also pass as fear and brands use this to help foster brand loyalty. Think of all those ads that have shown negative consequences for using the services of Company A instead of the shiny, comfortable Company B's offering that you already know and love.

Surprised makes us cling to things that bring us comfort.

Anger

Intense emotions such as anger and passion are what helps make content on the internet go viral. Strong emotions tend to elicit strong reactions - such as sharing of posts and engagement. Some studies have found that creating content to spark one's anger or anxiety has been shown to increase virality and increase the number of views your content receives. Be wary of this tactic as the attention you get may not be the attention you want.

Intense emotions lead to viral content and loyal followers.

Funny, inspiration or even sad pictures and videos aren't the only key to unlocking your target audiences' emotions during your marketing efforts. In fact, a large part of marketing means taking the psychology of colors into account.

Colors and Emotions

People tend to react differently to different colors and it's never just as simple as slapping content on a graphic and expecting it to go over well.

When you think about colors in marketing, the mind tends to lean toward graphics and social posts, but it doesn't end there. It's about the color of your logo, your website, the images attached to your blogs, it is everything to do with your business.

Have you noticed a similarity in websites and logos? Blues and greens remain among the most prevalent colors in branding.

Blue has been known to instill confidence in your potential clients and trust in your brand. It creates a calming, focused and professional view and is often favored amongst the legal industry, banks, financial advisors and other corporate industries.

Yet another prevalent color amongst businesses is green. The color green promotes a sensation of peacefulness, growth and health. It is also associated with wealth. As a result, the financial sector, science, government and HR companies tend to sway towards shades of green.

As a lawyer, you want to promote both feelings of trust and comfort so using those blues and greens may be in your best interest. The legal industry is typically viewed with a negative light and feelings of mistrust so many tend to gravitate towards shades of blue in their branding.

All About Blogging

Marketing takes on many different forms; one of which is blogging. This may be causing you to groan: "for law firms? Really?". Yes, really. There are many advantages of blogging, but we'll get to those in a minute.

When consulting with a marketing agency about SEO and/or lead generation, they may recommend blogging to you. Why? Because blogging has the power to help you rank higher and establish you as a thought leader in your practice area. It's a tool in a box of tools, and pretty near the top at that. And that's not all.

When working with lawyers marketing strategies, some of the most common questions we get are: Why should I blog? Can a blog really help my law firm grow? Can it help me rank higher in search engines? The short answer is yes, it can help with all of those when done correctly. Notice we used the term _correctly_, right?

Here's the deal, search engines love websites that are continually updated with new content. Sitting down to hammer out a blog when inspiration strikes is great. In fact, it's probably more than some of your competitors are doing. However, if you're not optimizing your blogs, they may not have the desired impact. Sure, it will help to establish you as an authority regardless but following some best practices can get you much more than that. If you're working hard to produce relevant and value-driven content, isn't it worth optimizing it to reap the most reward? Keep this in mind: You may be doing more than some of your competitors by producing content, but if you're not optimizing, you're not really competing.

What is blog optimization?

It's literally the same process as SEO really. Research keywords, write to include those keywords and the ideas they foster, ensure meta-data is well written, use an image, link to relevant inner pages of your website and other websites, and in some cases building links to your blog. Sharing or syndicating it on social media is also part of optimizing. Think of it like getting your kid dressed for kindergarten. You can't send your kid to school with a dirty shirt, and one shoe. Same thing applies here.

There are those that may prefer the stance of "it's not a competition". If you'd prefer to think of it another way, think of it like this. Creating content without optimizing means you MAY be able to rank on the search engines, but it's not likely to be very high - meaning you're the 47th result to show up for a specific keyword/keyphrase. That means that you're not on the first page, not even on page two or three of the search results. Let's look at some statistics:

According to HubSpot, there are 34,000 Google queries PER SECOND and over one trillion searches per month. That's a LOT of searches! Of those searches, 75 percent of users never go past the first page. What does this mean? That means that unless you're ranking on the first page for what your clients are looking for, you're not very visible. With all of that in mind, let's jump in.

In this chapter, we'll talk about:

• Ways blogging can help your law firm grow
• Review case studies
• 10 principles of blogging
• Determining whether your strategy is working

Benefits of Blogging

We talked about a couple of the benefits of blogging briefly already, but let's dive a bit deeper into the sea of benefit.

- Thought leader
- Relevant, value-driven content
- Drive traffic to your website
- Keywords/Search engine ranking
- Continuously updated content

Many law firms either don't have time or don't see the value in blogging and so often, don't take advantage.

Thought Leader

What is a thought leader?

A thought leader can be an individual or a business (such as your law firm) that is regarded by prospects, clients, associates and even competitors as a trusted source or authority within their respective practice areas. A thought leader offers unique advice, guidance and provides inspiration to others in their areas.

How do you become a thought leader?

If you're wondering how to become a thought leader in your practice area(s), you're not alone. Establishing yourself as a thought leader takes time and effort. You also can't just declare yourself a thought leader - the elusive title is one that is bestowed upon you. Continue to produce relevant and value-driven content and it will come. The more you write, the more you will rank. The more you rank in search, the more traffic you will get. The more web traffic you get from this relevant content, the more case files will be opened. The more this happens, the further your firm grows. You can use this content (the amount of quality of it) to position yourself more easily on professional associations panels, executive committees and boards. You are demonstrating, through blogging and writing that you are indeed the prolific "go to" in whatever topic you chose to write on. But let's not get totally over our skis. The important thing to remember is success begets success.

There is value in the early stages as well. You may not be an influencer or even well-known within your practice area, but that doesn't mean that the content you're producing is worthless. Your clients and potential clients want to know that you're an expert in your field - or at least competent enough that they can rely on your services. Which brings us to our next benefit.

Relevant, Value-Driven Content

It can take years to establish yourself as an expert to those in your practice area. Now we know the terms "expert" can be a dirty word in some states with respect to their bar associates. That really isn't the type of expert we are talking about. This type of expert isn't certified by anyone other than the public and perhaps your peers. We also know that to you, in the legal sense, you are chasing the respect of judges and opposing counsel, even those in your own firm. I want you to forget that for now. That is not necessarily relevant here.

See, it may take less time to prove yourself to your potential clients. Producing relevant, value-driven content for free can help your clients now and potential clients come to trust you. It can help to instill trust in those who are likely to need the help of you and your firm.

But how should you really be relevant? Write content

with this in mind: Understand your client's problems and provide the solutions. What are the questions people need answering when engaging your services? Start here and your content will be relevant.

Drive Traffic to Your Website

By producing relevant and value-driven content, such as blogs, you're providing a reason for people to visit your website AND to spend time there. Google Analytics is a beast and is also essential. If you haven't put a Google Analytics code on your website, you're behind the curve. That is a beast for another day, and we won't go into it in this book beyond telling you to install the code and talking about the bounce rate.

Some of the things you can monitor on Google Analytics is how much traffic your website is getting, when the busiest day and time of the week are, how many visits to each page and your bounce rate. Again, there is so much more that you could do, but we're not going to go into that in this book.

The bounce rate is the rate of visitors to your website who navigate away after viewing only one page. A higher bounce rate means that people aren't staying on your website and it may be a sign that you should consider restructuring your home page. If your website has a higher bounce rate, search engines like Google won't place much value in your website and it may cause you to rank lower. That said, don't be scared when your bounce rate is somewhere between 60-75%. The typical lawyers website is, and that's ok. It is somewhat unique to the business of law as an ecommerce store would never survive if 75% of it's traffic visited the home page and then left.

How can blogging help your bounce rate? Well, by providing content on your website, such as blogs, that provides engaging information that your audience would actually *want* to read, it will keep them on your website longer and decrease the bounce rate. Do we need to say that last part again??

Engaging content, such as a blog, entices users to spend more time on your website and therefore will decrease the bounce rate. That lower bounce rate will signal to the search engines that you are producing engaging content and may improve your ranking for certain keywords. Which leads us to our next subtopic.

Keywords and Search Engine Ranking
Look at keywords from this standpoint:

You are a potential client who is looking to find a new dentist. Perhaps you've asked a friend for a referral and then looked them up online to get their contact info and check out their reviews. Maybe you've just gone straight to the search engine. Either way, at some point we end up at the search engine. What do you do now? You type in a keyword or keyphrase to bring up results that are relevant to your query. For this example, let's say you typed in "family dentist in Orlando, FL who uses nitrous".

If there are let's say 10,000 people searching for those exact keywords every single month and your website doesn't come up in those searches, you are not competing for clients. You're not even in the running. Not even in the bandstands. You will most likely _not_ be found by those 10k people who are looking for a family dentist in Orlando.

This is where we tell you that you need to do your homework. You need to find out what words and phrases your potential clients are querying and make sure they're on your website - and we don't mean one and done. While you should still conduct research on what people are querying, you should also check out what your competitors are doing. This can provide you a great jumping off point.

The trick is to make sure that they appear natural and that you aren't over optimizing your content in there. Keyword stuffing can negatively impact your search engine ranking. There are loads of tools out there that can help you accomplish your keyword research - some free, most paid.

If you need a refresher on keyword research, hop back over to that chapter. But those blogging purposes, you should be including keywords in your title. So, if you are an estate planning attorney, it can be helpful to think of the most popular questions your new clients ask you in a consult. Something like "How long will it take to complete the probate process in Whittier, California? See what we did there?

Continuously Updated Content
Bottom Line Up Front (BLUF): Websites who do not continually provide fresh content will be viewed as static websites (aka dead) by the search engines as you aren't offering up anything new.

The search engines use bots to crawl your website. The newer content your website provides, the more your website will be indexed. This does *not* mean that you will rank higher simply based on frequent indexing. It means that you'll have more *opportunities* to rank higher.

Google has over 200 factors that go into determining how

well your website will rank in the search engines and it's all really a balancing act. Is your website credible? Does your content have the right blend of keywords? What is your website's authority? While you may feel like your answer to all of those is yes, what do the numbers tell you? How many keywords are you ranking for? How many quality backlinks does your website have? Are you producing relevant and engaging content to drive traffic?

Case Studies

The benefits of blogging are there, for sure, but not without a fair bit of effort. So, if you're going to make the effort, you'll probably want to know that it works before investing your time (and money if you're paying someone to do it for you) in blogging.

I shared this with a group of attorneys in Virginia at a Virginia Trial Lawyers lunch and learn just how well blogging coupled with SEO worked during COVID-19.

"When COVID first hit we had a client in mid-town Manhattan literally go dark. Because courts were suddenly shuttered. With 8 attorneys on their staff, everyone had time to fill. So, we put them to work writing family law blog content related to COVID. We covered the gamut of what to do if your co-parent has COVID (do you still send your child to their house) to how to get along in quarantine with a spouse you know you want to divorce. Within days, we had 18-20 pieces published on the site. We have never posted new content for one client this quickly, so it was a real challenge for our team to maintain SEO integrity while essentially rushing this content. Within a week of publishing this content, we saw traffic literally double. We had national rank for COVID/divorce keywords and even out ranked major NYC news outlets and other national sites. While we don't want national traffic on the site per se, the traffic was mostly New Yorkers doing national broad keyword type searches. Google wasn't yet algorithmically caught up, so we immediately benefited. Months later, the site's traffic has stayed at those new levels, so it wasn't just a flash in the pan. The search engines were hungry for content, we fed them."

Okay I am ready to blog, but now what? Read the10 Principles of Blogging

As with everything, there are some best practices, or principles, to blogging.

Let's take a look at the 10 principles of blogging.

1. *Define Your Target Audience* - Not everyone is your client. Write to those who are likely to convert to clients. What common interests do your clients have?

2. *Conduct Topic Research* - Seasons change, the economy goes through hardships, and every once in a while, a major event such as a pandemic occurs. Stay ahead of the curve by researching what topics are relent <u>at that time</u>.

3. *Conduct Keyword Research* - We already talked about this one and why it's important. Have a look at what keywords you'd like your website to rank higher for and try to shape your blog around them.

4. *Inbound and Outbound Links* - Inbound links are links in your article (or other section of your website) that link to other articles or sections of your website. Outbound links refer to links that go to other websites. As a general rule of thumb, you should have at least

one or two of each in your article. Now, you're not just throwing a random URL in there, you're highlighting a word and then hyperlinking the word(s) to the inbound or outbound URL.

5. *SEO Formatting* - You can't escape SEO formatting! Just like the rest of your page, your blog or article should include a title, which will be your H1 tag (Heading Tag AKA H-Tag), and your subtitles which will be your H2, H3 and H4 tags. These tags are important as they help the search engine determine how to index your website. If the search engines get confused, you won't rank as high even if you've met all of the other factors in their algorithm.

6. *Minimum Word Count* - It's tempting to just throw a couple of paragraphs out there, but you should aim for a minimum of about 600 words. If you can, aim higher. While 600 words would have been enough to rank in prior years, these days you really need to have about 1500+ words to be competitive with those appearing on page one of the search engines.

7. *Ensure Readability* - Write to your reader. Many law firms write as if they were writing to other professionals in the legal industry. What do I mean by that? Lawyers often have difficulty conveying a message that those of us without a background in law could really understand. That is often jokingly called "legalese". You've got to find a way of translating that legalese into a way that those without a background in your practice area can understand. *When writing your blogs, you want to make sure that your readers can fully understand what you're putting out there. In addition to that, you want to put your best foot forward*

by ensuring your post is free of spelling and grammatical errors.

8. *Keep Opinions To Yourself & Avoid Controversial Topics* - It's tempting to join in those hot topics surrounding controversial issues, politics, or to express your opinion. Save that for your personal (and private) lives. Unless your business' brand is built around a certain controversial issue, you run the risk of alienating a percentage of your potential clients. Even worse, participating in a controversial issue may make your firm go viral for all the wrong reasons, which could lead to you being forced to close shop.

9. *Be Objective* - Dial down the sales pitch. We've all gotten called by some pushy salespeople who can't take no for an answer. Don't be that pushy salesperson. To really build your brand and a loyal following, provide them with relevant and valuable information less the sales pitch. It's okay to conclude your blog with a call to action, but you shouldn't be ramming your "buy now" pitch down their throats. You may be a lawyer on top of your game, but eventually your pushiness will be enough to drive them away.

   Being objective also means being unbiased. Of course, you'll be biased towards your own services, but on the topic you are writing you should refrain from taking sides.

10. *Promote It!* - You just wrote a kick a$$ blog! Go out there and tell the world!! Share your blog on social media. Consider pushing your blogs out to Facebook, LinkedIn, Twitter, Instagram AND Google My Business. Not all of those will be relevant to all

industries. Google My Business is a great way to put information out there, especially blogs, but is often underutilized for that purpose. It's free, your business should already have a GMB profile, so why not?! It's just one more way for you to drive traffic to your website.

Determining Whether Blogging is Working

Blogging is the long-haul game. There are no overnight success options and anyone who tells you otherwise is lying to you. Realistically, if your website's SEO is in good shape and you've optimized your website with the appropriate keywords and keyphrases, including your blog section, you're looking at about four to six months on average to start seeing results. Don't be discouraged. Keep working on your keywords and producing relevant, continuous content and your hard work will pay off.

Let's set some realistic expectations here as well. In four to six months when you start seeing results, you're most likely *not* going to be on page one. You may not even be hitting page two or three, but if you're in the top 50 you're going somewhere! When you start ranking for those keywords, keep building on them to continually improve your ranking. Remember that your competitors are still out there hustling. If you don't keep up with them or let your content grow stagnant, you'll lose any ground you've gained.

Here are some metrics you can use to measure some of the items we've talked about in this chapter.

Domain Authority (DA) is a ranking metric created by a software company called Moz. Moz has some really great - a couple free - tools on their website. One of those free tools is the link explorer. This tool will show you your DA and some of the factors that it took into account to give you that ranking. It will show you how your DA has changed over time, every link that links back to your website (backlinks), how many inbound links you have, how many and what keywords your website is ranking for, etc.

In addition to Moz, there are several other tools out there that you can use to track how you're ranking for keywords - most of them are paid. One of our favorite's is Rank Ranger. This tool offers quite a number of capabilities, including the ability to track keyword rank AND to conduct keyword research.

While you're checking out your own link in Moz, check out your competitor's website as well to give you some idea of links you could try to get a backlink from or even keywords you should be trying to rank for.

Selecting Effective Attorney Blog Topics

Hopefully after the last chapter you can recognize the value in blogging. One of the most difficult but first steps when determining what to blog about, is selecting effective attorney blog topics. Sit back and shake off that stress, you have enough of that running your law practice. Remember that the end game is the benefit of improving a firm's organic search engine placement while answering questions consumers may have about your law practice. The posted articles you will write will have a much more lasting effect than "throwing" money at Google as part of a PPC campaign. Blogs are indexed by search engines. Further, the articles provide a way of building credibility with potential clients who visit your site with genuine legal issues and concerns. When articles are written on legitimately unique and engaging topics, they can appear at or near the top for certain search terms for years. By the same token, content that is generic or un-engaging typically will not be effective in terms of attracting traffic or converting traffic into calls and emails from potential clients.

Four Types of Effective Attorney Blog Topics

Frequently Asked Questions (FAQ): Blogs that provide answers to frequently asked questions can be extremely effective especially when they focus on specific topics.

For example, an FAQ dealing with what steps to take in the immediate aftermath of a car accident will tend to be more helpful to consumers than a blog with a broader more generic focus like "Personal Injury FAQs." FAQs can address the exact types of questions posed by potential clients, so when new visitors come to your site, you increase the probability of addressing specific concerns. This ability to provide preliminary answers to potential clients' legal questions will tend to spur client calls. FAQs also are useful because there are a virtually unlimited supply of topic specific FAQs that can be posted on your website. Since developing topics that are interesting and helpful is one of the most difficult parts of blogging, FAQs can provide a wealth of informative posts.

Firm/Personal Accomplishments: While important firm accomplishments, seminars or significant case results can provide effective blog topics that build value with clients, this type of blogging requires subtlety. Clients dismiss blogs that appear to be mostly self-aggrandizing. When writing blog posts covering these types of topics, it is important to connect the topic to consumers. For example, an announcement of your completion of a seminar for specialists might discuss significant new legal developments that could affect clients. While the goal of the blog might be to make clients aware that you actively work to stay current regarding changes in the law, the tone of the blog should be about sharing valuable information that you have learned with clients. If you have been certified as a specialist in your area of law or recognized on a website for your accomplishments, you should explain the standards or requirements for specialty status or inclusion on a list for recognition. If you are reviewing a successful case result, you will want to report the favorable outcome, but the focus should be on issues in the case that impact other clients.

Novel Changes in the Law: When significant court decisions or statutory enactments/amendments occur, these changes can constitute an excellent topic for blogs provided the issues affect potential clients. Highly technical changes that do not impact a significant number of people will have only limited appeal. Any blog discussing actual cases or statutory changes should be written in plain English that demonstrates both your mastery of the subject and ability to communicate complex legal issues to laypeople in an understandable and straightforward way.

When writing these kinds of blogs, you will want to break away from the "legalese", if you will. Remember that your audience (aka potential clients) aren't going to understand that kind of talk - otherwise they would likely be representing themselves! It is totally fine to cite case law, link out to it and all that, but make sure that you've worded everything in a way that anyone can understand.

Most Common Practice Area Issues: Since the objective of attorney blogging is to attract the maximum number of readers who might end up retaining a lawyer, the most common types of issues handled by the firm can provide a consistent stream of topics. If you are a personal injury attorney that handles construction accidents, for example, you might write a blog about third-party lawsuits as a supplement to worker's compensation benefits. Similarly, family law blogs that include suggestions for dealing with high conflict custody disputes or parental move-away issues will likely target the specific types of clients a family lawyer wishes to attract. Essentially, this approach involves working backwards by starting with an idea of the specific clients you want to attract and writing blogs that include issues relevant to that type of client.

This particular topic area is a great one. Seriously. It's a great way to not only provide valuable information to your audience on a topic that they're actually querying for, but also to hit on those SEO keywords to help you rank higher. Though, really, with all blogs regardless of topic should be optimized with your SEO keywords.

Using Google Trends to Source Topic Ideas

Often overlooked, Google Trends is a free tool that you can use to find ideas for your blog topics. There are some widespread trends across the practice areas that occur every year in seasonal trends. For instance, if your practice area is family law there are a few times of the year that people query for divorce attorneys and divorce topics more than others.

Here's the link:
https://trends.google.com/trends/?geo=US

You have the ability to go in there, armed with a few particular keywords - not necessarily your SEO keywords - and look for trends that you could write on. Let's say we want to look at when divorce terms may be more prevalent.

We begin our query by typing in "divorce". Now, you have the option to select from a number of different types. The two types you'll want to play around with here are search term and topic. For this example, we'll use search terms.

Once you've clicked on the appropriate result, your screen might look similar to this. At the top of that screen, you'll want to set up some parameters, unless you are scoping out national trends. Where it says "United States" you'll want to toggle that and select your geographic area that you practice out of. If you're querying trends for blog topics, one year isn't enough to show a trend, so toggle that "past 12 months" to include at least two years worth of data, if not more.

Next to your keyword, you can also include other search terms or topics by clicking on "Compare".

Once you do that, you'll be able to look at the spikes and compare dates. Do spikes in data occur during specific times each year? That indicates that this topic would be a great fit for that particular time frame.

Play around with different keyword searches, look at competitors blog topics, but more importantly GET WRITING!

Guest Blogging for Law Firms

Why guest posting for your law firm, is the worst SEO idea since sliced bread was first cut?

It finally happened. I say finally, because for literally years now I have been bombarded with emails from clients and pretend marketers soliciting our clients for guest blogging. Every single time, after using a little common sense, explained to clients why this is a horrible idea, and denied other marketers' access to our sites. I recently talked about this with Mordy Oberstein at Rank Ranger on his podcast, you should give it a listen when it drops on July 7th. While Mordy agreed with my stance, the concept of guest blogging has been a controversial one. As a marketer, I look at my job with an extreme necessity to be risk averse. If I think there may be an issue with a SEO technique, even if widely used by others, I run from it. Not to get into the weeds, but there is always an SEO shiny new penny. Everyone has heard of black hat SEO, that's not what I am talking about. We call these techniques ``gray hat" because Google has not flatly come out against them, or even acknowledged them as helpful; though sear optimizers often look at the data and see it differently.

What is guest blogging in legal marketing anyway?

Before explaining the digital equivalent, let's look at this in terms of old school brick and mortar marketing.

Remember when you used to go to a restaurant and there was a cork board with business cards on it? You may have grabbed one for a gardener or home repair company there at one point in your life. No, this is not guest blogging. But, what if you were in the middle of a conversation while ordering and the waitress overhears you need a gardener for your new house and says something like "We use blossom tree service at my house, and they are great". You think, cool, I will give them a call. You ask for their number and weigh the endorsement based off of her positive words. The referral was made, and it carried weight back in the day, didn't it? Let's take this one step further here and say that this restaurant you were in served only breakfast. The waitress heard you planning your lunch and recommended Bob's Burgers (not to be confused with the popular off-color TV show). This is akin to guest blogging. Let's put this into legal marketing terms. The process of guest blogging is placing YOUR content onto another law firm's website, linking back to yours. This other law firm also posts THEIR content onto yours. It's the digital equivalent of endorsing another law firm, usually without ever knowing them.

Seems harmless, what's the big deal?

Well, on the surface, not much. And that is where things go wrong. Enterprising and unscrupulous bad actors run rampant in the SEO space and will do anything to take advantage of what could be a great thing, and ruin it for the rest of us. As an attorney, you have many colleagues you would be fine endorsing. So maybe you write a blog about divorce and place it onto your colleague's personal injury law firm site's website. You link between the sites and call it day. If you truly know each other, and are within the same geographic region, then I don't see a huge problem with that. But now think about a marketing agency that used this technique at scale for all of their clients, and you are one of them. Links between law firm websites all of the country being interlinked and linked to in an unnatural way, is a very bad thing. You are literally endorsing an attorney you know nothing about. On your website. Officially, and formally.

Why does Google care? And why should you? Is Google penalizing for these posts?

One of the largest hurdles to overcome as a legal SEO agency is figuring out which websites to build authoritative off-site links back to our client's websites. You have to identify the website you are going to publish an article on, write the article, send to the client to gain approval, deal with edits and rewrites, then submit it, submit the image to be used, request the link, check the link for correctness, post on social and more. It's a time-consuming arduous task at best.

There are only a handful of companies that claim to have solved this issue for agencies like us; none of which we trust. One such promising enterprise recently launched a new product at SEMRush; an industry leading SEO reporting tool. They were offering building out guest post links by matching publishers up to high quality relevant sites as an outreach service, which was days later shelved after Google warned "they don't help site rank". Was this tortious interference you may ask? I say maybe, but to my knowledge there has yet to be any filings on the matter. Yet. Soon after, speculation ensued about a potential for a manual action or penalty, which has not come.

As a thought leader in the legal marketing space, I keep my eye on not only what Google is saying, but also what they aren't saying, and what they are doing. You have to watch your own data, and the data of others. I have noticed in their few public releases and tweets from their liaison's is the word "natural". They are consistently and uniformly using this word to describe what you should be writing about, linking to and generally engaging in from an SEO perspective. Be natural. If there should be a link, and it's natural, make the link. Google algorithms are focused on trying to read your content and judge its material worth to rank for a given search. Guest posting is not natural at all, in any way. Posting content on someone's website 16 states away from where your business address is, that Google can clearly determine from your GMB listings, sees a reference in your text and so on is not natural. In fact, if you were writing code to look at the validity of a link within content, wouldn't this be one of the easiest signals to look at? Location? Absolutely.

Google's John Mueller, who I don't always think is being straight with us in his tweets, has said some pretty damning, straight forward things about this subject. In one tweet he says ``The part that's problematic is the links — if you're providing the content/the links, then those links shouldn't be passing signals & should have the rel-sponsored / rel-nofollow attached..."

Replying to @MarkPreston1969

The part that's problematic is the links -- if you're providing the content/the links, then those links shouldn't be passing signals & should have the rel-sponsored / rel-nofollow attached. It's fine to see it as a way of reaching a broader audience.

8:36 AM · Jun 11, 2020 · TweetDeck

Then he goes on to say:

"Essentially if the link is within the guest post, it should be nofollow, even if it's a "natural" link you're adding there.

FWIW none of this is new, and I'm not aware of any plans to ramp up manual reviews of this. We catch most of these algorithmically anyway."

John
@JohnMu

Replying to @bike_gremlin and @MarkPreston1969

Essentially if the link is within the guest post, it should be nofollow, even if it's a "natural" link you're adding there.

FWIW none of this is new, and I'm not aware of any plans to ramp up manual reviews of this. We catch most of these algorithmically anyway.

2:53 AM · Jun 13, 2020 · TweetDeck

The key item he mentions there to me is, "We catch most of these algorithmically anyway". That's code for: don't waste your time buddy. Time, effort and client's money. Even when these articles are clearly labeled as guest posts or sponsored, they are still problematic.

Are these links potentially illegal?

Building these types of links can be easy. There are TONS of website publishers out there that email me on an on-going basis offering these links. Many of them, anomalous, unlabeled and some don't last longer than a few months. But, according to the Federal Trade Commission's guidelines about "native advertising", it might just be illegal:

"A basic truth-in-advertising principle is that it's deceptive to mislead consumers about the commercial nature of content. Advertisements or promotional messages are deceptive if they convey to consumers expressly or by implication that they're independent, impartial, or from a source other than the sponsoring advertiser – in other words, that they're something other than ads. "

You, as a publisher of your law firm's website may be held accountable to label native advertising as ads or advertising. Wouldn't it be lovely being on the receiving end of a federal lawsuit from the FTC? All because of your SEO agency? No wonder I take my job as a law firm marketer so serious.

What should/can you do? Does your law firm have these links built without you even knowing about it?

The short answer is you absolutely can. If you have had an SEO agency build you links over the years, and a lot of you have, then you absolutely might. But how do you find them? Start by asking your current marketing provider if they engage in guest blogging on your behalf, and if they do, to please remove all of the content with links on your website and others they would have posted it on.

Go to your own website and look for blogs and content from other law firms. If you see authors you don't recognize, then you are on the right track. You can take a look at your backlink profile using tools like SpyFu, Ahref's or Majestic, but if you are going down that road, you might want to hire a professional to help you out.

Leveraging Trending Topics

We all know that there is no cookie cutter approach to legal marketing. Not only is every industry vastly different, every business unique, but there are also several other key factors that can influence a law firms' marketing strategy. No matter the industry; economics and politics can always play a factor in business. It's getting ahead of those trending topics that can not only drive more traffic your way, but also establish you as a thought leader (and a leader in general) on the subject. Establishing yourself as a thought leader on a trending topic can also drive attention to your law firm from news outlets, giving your firm a significant amount of exposure.

As an Attorney, What is Content Marketing?

First, let's answer the question... What is content marketing from a lawyers perspective? Content marketing is a marketing method that involves the creation and dissemination of content such as blogs, videos, social media posts, etc. with the intent of engaging with current and potential clients.

So, how can this help your law firm gain traction? Getting in front of trending topics sets you apart from your competitors and can even get you some free publicity. Let's look at current events in our area for example. Today, January 20th, there is a large rally, organized by the Virginia Citizens Defense League, that is expected to draw thousands of armed protestors in response to proposed gun legislation many feel infringes on the second amendment.

For a law firm who focuses on criminal defense in Virginia, this topic is particularly important. Not only could the bills change current laws in Virginia, which is important for criminal defense law firms, but it is also a highly searched subject on the internet. Enter law firm blogging.

Driving Traffic to Your Website

Blogging (on your own website or blog) for law firms can be a great way to set yourself apart from your competitors and also to drive potential clients to your website. How? Most of the free (non-paid) traffic coming to your website is from a Google search. Always remember that Google's job is to show the most relevant search results it can to its "customers"; searchers. Let's use our example of Virginia's gun legislation. Thousands and thousands of people from all over the United States are querying search engines like Google, using keywords related to gun legislation and rallies in Virginia. Optimizing your blogs on the topic with the right keywords can make your blog show in their search results when they are querying the topic, thus driving traffic/potential clients to your website. Here's another added advantage – many will shy away from a controversial topic such as the ongoing legislation and 2A sanctuaries popping up, but presented in the right manner can set you apart in a big way.

Establishing Your Law Firm as a Thought Leader

Another way blogging, and really content marketing as a whole, can boost your marketing strategy is by establishing yourself as a thought leader on the topic. While this is just as important for everyday topics relating to your practice areas, this is especially important for trending issues – just like the current proposed gun legislation. This can really set you apart from your competitors who are probably waiting for the dust to settle (if at all) to inform readers of what's going on. When individuals (and news outlets) are searching for articles on a topic and your firm shows in their results, this can help establish you as a thought leader on the subject.

Public Relations

Getting ahead of a trending topic can also align your firm for some free public relations (though not guaranteed). Law firm blogging with the right keywords may help news outlets find your article and contact you for a quote or an appearance on a news segment. This is especially important if you're writing on a trending topic such as the gun legislation example. Of course, not all PR comes organically. Connecting with the right PR person can help get your firm in the spotlight as well.

Things to Avoid

Just as much as law firm blogging can establish your firm as a thought leader and drive traffic to your website, it can also harm your reputation if you aren't careful. We're all human and we all have our own personal feelings on a subject and sometimes, those feelings are shown in blogs or social media postings.

When dealing with a trending topic such as gun legislation, it is very easy to get swept up. It is a topic that sparks emotions and incites passion. Choosing one side over the other can draw negative attention to your law firm and can limit your future clientele. It is important to keep emotions and opinions out of your content marketing. Stick to presenting the facts for the best possible outcome.

Bonus: Using Google Trends

When it comes to identifying trending topics, of course, economics will play a huge role - take 2020 for example. In addition to economics, there will be seasonal trends for everything - and the legal industry is no exception here.

To help you identify trending topics to leverage in your marketing, you can use Google Trends, a free tool available to everyone -> https://trends.google.com

In a recent report put out by Precision Legal Marketing, we were able to use Google Trends to help identify both 2020 trends and overall/seasonal trends for various practice areas (*see https://www.precisionlegalmarketing.com/blog to read the full report*). Check out this example:

Virginia Employment Law Trends Analysis

A Look at 2020

With the closure of many businesses across the nation came an insurmountable number of people who are suddenly unemployed. For businesses that furloughed only a percentage of their staff, how did they make the determination on who they were going to let go and who would stay on?

While looking at the 12 month overview below may show that there were periods of 2020 that were higher than the rest for wrongful termination, they fall primarily during the beginning of the year (January) and in the summer months (peaking in July). What's interesting to note here is that for wrongful termination, 2020 has been a relatively tame year in comparison. We'll go into that a bit more in the next section.

Many businesses across the nation were allowed by their respective states to reopen in mid to late May and June on a phased reopening plan (well, at least for the majority of the states). If you look at the June 14th mark on the chart below you can see an uptick in the number of wrongful termination queries, workplace discrimination queries, workplace harassment queries and employment lawyer queries. This indicates that as businesses were allowed to reopen, workplace issues resumed as well.

Let's look at the charts.

That image was a screenshot from Google Trends.

You see, using this data, we're able to identify a multitude of things. For instance, based on the information in that graphic, we can see an increase in users querying Google for employment law related search terms, particularly more so around November/December time.

So, if your law firm practices employment law as at least one of your practice areas, perhaps you'd want to consider shifting your content to focus on those search terms during the times it typically peaks annually. And this same method can be applied to all practice areas.

And it doesn't just end at diving into specific practice areas.

We're bringing COVID-19 up again here... Who could have predicted the full scope of what would happen when COVID-19 was officially declared a global pandemic? Those are things that you can't really prepare for. However, law firms who adapted quickly and shifted their strategy to encompass COVID-19 potential and current impacts on their respective practice areas were able to dominate the search engines, garnering loads of page one ranking for trending and relevant keywords *that people were actually querying for*. These law firms not only stayed afloat during the pandemic but actually doubled, if not tripled, their client intake during this time.

All About Press Releases

If you're building a public relations strategy for your law firm (or looking for a link to boost your DA and SEO), you might have considered writing and issuing a press release. Though many people know what a press release is, very few know when and how to use them.

Read on to learn what exactly a press release is, the purpose behind releasing one, and tips to writing a profound press release.

What is a Press Release?

A press release is a written communication document that reports brief but specific information to the media. The information is usually related to an event, product launch, or any other newsworthy happening that requires press coverage. It is also great for obtaining quick keyword ranking and a valuable backlink.

The one to three pager document is circulated among media groups, with the hopes that newscasters, reporters, and editors will use the information in an upcoming radio or TV broadcast, or print it in a magazine or newspaper issue, and also on the media's webpage. Press releases are tied to an organization or a law firm (really any business) and are delivered to the media through various means.

Purpose of a Press Release

The chief use of a press release is to promote a piece of significant and specific information clearly. Numerous situations might call for the issuance of a press release, such as:

Firm Announcement: Expansion, restructuring, new locations, relocation, new investors or financial partners, strategic partnerships are all newsworthy press releases.

Employee Announcement: Significant promotions and new hires are worthy of a press release.

Public Announcement: If there is any information that holds prominent significance or value for the public, issuing a press release would be an appropriate medium.

Awards or Honors: Special recognition or awards the firm or it's members have earned are prime for a press release. Accolades like Superlawyers, Martindale-Hubbell AV awards and alike should all be worthy candidates for a release.

Initiative Announcement: New external or internal projects that may have a considerable impact on the organization's community would be suitable for a press release. A new charitable cause or that golf tournament you are sponsoring.

Notable Case Results: Large jury verdicts in personal injury cases, large civil litigation settlements, noteworthy criminal court acquittals are all perfect candidates.

Beyond that, a press release adheres to a strict format and serves three promotional and marketing purposes:

- To inform the media about an event with the hope that they'll spread the word.
- To share something about your firm, hoping a newsperson will see a story in your press release and create an actual news article about it.
- To promote your law firm on the internet via social networks, blogs, and websites.

The most fundamental question to ask yourself before preparing a press release is, 'who cares about this information?'; as long as the answer encompasses individuals who will go to press for this information or read it, know that you're on the right track of issuing the press release. On the contrary, if the only people who will be interested in the information are your employees, friends, or family, you do not really require a public press release.

Key Features of a Press Release

To make it clear to reporters, editors, and writers that the information you provide them is a press release and not a letter to the editor or an advertisement, make sure you send it in a press release format. Here are some key features of a press release:

Media Contact Information: In the upper left or right corner, make sure to add the media contact information, i.e., name, email address, and the phone number of the person who the individuals should reach out to in case they have any follow-up queries.

Release Date: Below media contact information, add the date on which the report can be made public. For urgent announcements, write 'for immediate release' instead of the date. Similarly, for future releases, write 'embargoed until (add required date).'

Highlight Topic: On the left side or center of the page, write a topic headline that encapsulates the press release information. For example, 'Jack Matthews Promoted to General Partner.'

Body of the Press Release: On the first line of the release, add the name of your city and state name in bold format and the date on which you are making the statement. For example, 'CHICAGO, ILLINOIS – May 27, 2021'. The next step is to start the announcement and encompass all the necessary information.

Write the announcement in an inverted pyramid style, mention the most essential information in the first sentence and the second most important in the next. This allows the editor to edit material from the bottom while ensuring all the crucial aspects are included.

Double Space Paragraphs: Make sure to double space the paragraphs and end the content with '###' symbols in the bottom of the center of your release.

A well-written press release, sent to the right media for publication can yield thousands and even tens of thousands of dollars' worth of free publicity, especially where the stakes are high for the firm or it's client(s).

4 Tips for Writing a Press Release

Tip #1: A press release should incorporate an *attention-grabbing headline* and should always be written in the third person.

Tip #2: Make your information interesting and exciting by linking it to an ongoing trend, that doesn't always have to be something legal. Nobody likes to read a monotonous piece of writing.

Tip #3: Avoid using rigid and dry wording if you do not want to lose your audience with the first sentence. A yawn-worthy press release would do you no benefit.

Tip #4: Your press release must not be just a recitation of facts. Include quotes by prominent figures attending the event. Doing this can act as a rhetorical device to increase the interest level of the readers.

It is crucial to understand that a press release is not a definite marketing tool. Do not expect the media to jump on each press release you write. But do not give up either. Sustained and continuous efforts pave the way to achieve fruitful publicity and press releases are a vital component of a PR strategy. Thus, keep searching for ways to make your release stand out and gain enormous media coverage.

What should you do with your press release now that it's written? Where do you send it?

Great questions! Once you've written your press release, the next thing to do is to release it. There are a number of outlets out there that you can submit your press release through that will range in price. Here are a few places that we recommend you check out:

https://www.pr.com/

https://kisspr.com/

The paid ones like the two listed above are great because they normally publish your press release within a short amount of time and you get some really great backlinks to further help improve your Domain Authority.

Check out the back of the book for *81 FREE Sites to Post Your Press Release*! (*Note: The free sites often do not give **dofollow** backlinks. This means that in terms of SEO and building your domain authority, those links will **not** help you.*)

Once you've decided where you would like to post your press release, the next step is to review their submission guidelines. This is an important step to submitting your press release so make sure you actually read them. If your post does not meet their guidelines, they likely will not send it out. The guidelines will tell you everything from the type of content they accept to format, length and more.

If your post meets their guidelines, you're ready to publish. In addition to providing your article, you'll also need to provide your contact information and in some cases a royalty free image.

Is promoting your firm with video worth it?

I bet you were just wondering when we were going to talk about video marketing. We place video under the content section of this book because it truly is content marketing, just in the form of a video.

In the realm of digital marketing, video has been viewed as a must-have to maximize your content marketing efforts. But like any marketing effort, just because you're utilizing the medium doesn't mean that you're going to get the ROI you expect.

Like any content being produced, whether it's a blog post, article, white-paper or even a status update on a social media outlet – quality content that is relevant to the audience is going to be the goal. Video is no different. IF you have a quality video that hits home with your target audience, your chance of obtaining a higher ROI is much improved.

Look at it this way…not everyone likes the same TV shows, right? Some folks like mystery, others prefer action, while others like the classics.

If you are producing a video for your firm, what level of entertainment and value are you providing so they will pay attention to what you have to offer? Your firm's video would need to seriously stand out in the crowd of well over 500 videos of other firms that are just like it. If your intent is to sit behind a desk and free form talk, you may want to not waste your time.

A Guide to Video Marketing – What is it? Benefits & Tips for Success

Video marketing has exploded over the past few years, and it is only going to escalate in the future. Several research pieces have shown that people retain 20 percent of what they read, 10 percent of what they hear, and 80 percent of what they see.

Videos, when used in the right way, can be a perfect communication tool for law firms. If done correctly, it can lead to increased leads, website traffic, and consumer engagement. Should we reference the other chapter?

And the best part is that developing an effective video marketing strategy does not have to be complicated. The key to success is to have a concrete plan and content for your video before you start.

But what is video marketing?

What is Video Marketing?

If a picture is worth a thousand words, then how much more valued is a video? That is the foundation of video marketing, a straightforward marketing strategy that incorporates engaging videos into the law firm's marketing campaign.

Video marketing is used for a plethora of reasons, from

building client relationships to promoting your service. Moreover, video marketing also serves as a medium to promote customer testimonials, present how-to's, deliver viral content, and live-stream events.

In simple terms, when a law firm uses a video to market its brand or service, educates current or prospective clients, interacts, and engages with them on social media channels, that is a form of video marketing.

How Video Marketing Works?

The 'how' of video marketing seems pretty simple on the surface: law firms develop a video to promote their firm, raise awareness of their services, drive conversions, and foster client engagement. But in practice, it is a lot more complicated than this. Like many other legal marketing efforts, meaningful data is required to drive video marketing. Thus, law firms must observe and monitor multiple metrics to track customer engagement.

To build your video marketing strategy, you must:

Allocate Resources:

You will be required to designate some budget for the video – decent equipment, a video marketing team or guru, and good editing software– and the time to create it.

Tell Your Story:

Storytelling might have never been as vital as it is in video marketing, thus start brainstorming. Figure out what stories you want to tell and how you will share them with the target audience.

Engage Audience:

It is not enough to just share your stories; you must also

endeavor to foster customer engagement during the process. What will hook your target audience? How will you make the stories interesting?

Shorter is Better:

There is no fixed length for marketing videos, but the rule of thumb shows that shorter is better. Hence, be ruthless with the editing. Cut out anything that is extraneous as attention spans nowadays are short, thus make the best of what you got.

Publish:

Once the video is ready, make sure you publish it far and wide. Embed them on your website, upload on YouTube, and on all your other social media channels.

Analyze: Focus on stats and track metrics to determine which video performs the best and why.

How Video Marketing Benefit Law Firms

Few of the many benefits provided by video marketing to law firms are:

Improved Conversion Rates

Including meaningful videos on a landing page can boost conversion by 80 percent according to HubSpot. Obviously that stat depends upon what type of landing page it is. Watching a convincing presenter in a video can influence customers' buying behavior and compel a visitor to turn into a lead or turn a convert into a client, compared to simply reading the same information alone.

Videos for SEO

Search engines keep looking for content that has viewer

engagement capacity. YouTube is the second leading search engine behind Google. If you put a video on your website and YouTube, your opportunity and visibility to show up in search engines may be significantly increased. It is important to note that "video seo" is a professional service, and is something that must be done the right way. Uploading a video to youtube is only part of the equation, but not stopping the good for the pursuit of perfection is worth mentioning.

Foster Credibility and Trust

Videos are a great way to create a distinct personality for your brand or firm as it enables you to bond and connect with your audience and earn their trust. Potential clients can only see pictures of you on your website. Giving a video and voice to that image can be powerful. Remember, people hire attorneys and not 'law firms" so showing them WHO they will be hiring is very powerful.

Encourage Social Shares

This is the age of viral videos, and according to Hub-Spot, 92 percent of mobile video users share videos with other people. This is an excellent opportunity to have fun and show what your firm is all about. Thus, come up with video content that is relevant to your target audience, or practice area. In these videos, encourage people to share on social media, like, subscribe and pass on to friends. Be direct.

Video Marketing Tips for Success

Tip #1: Have a Purpose

Making videos has become so much simpler that people often forget some basics. Thus, make sure that your video has a substantial purpose. Write an outline about your videos content point by point. Use the old adage of "tell em what you are going to tell them, then tell them, then tell them again what you told them. Pre planning prevents poor performance. So while you shouldn't read from a script, you may want to write one out. It will help organize your thoughts and keep you on message.

Tip #2: Always Include a CTA

Always try to include some introductory text in your videos that should lead to a call to action. CTA's set up the viewer's expectation for the main content of the video. This needs to be something direction like "if you are in need of divorce, you should call our firm". Then proceed to tell them WHY.

Tip #3: Set a Video Theme

Video marketing is likely to be more successful when each video is based on a single purpose. If you feel you must include more than one topic in a single video, then try to formulate a common thread between all the different issues. Always remember that the video should serve and fulfill one ultimate purpose.

Tip #4: Don't Pitch for Clients

Generally, videos are not the place or the medium to make a sales pitch. If done the right way, the video itself will help to drive sales. But the main aim should be to offer the target audience with clear information they need to understand the product or service and ultimately lead them further into the sales funnel.

Video marketing is an excellent tool for effective communication in this digital age, especially when the span of attention of people is rapidly decreasing.

There are some really great (and affordable) tools out there to help you create some amazing videos from explainers and promotional to whiteboard and cartoons.

So, if you decide to produce a video for your firm, how can you stand out? Be unique. Some final thoughts...

As an example, we produced 24 video testimonial videos and stitched them together into practice areas and placed them into a video book with a 10-inch screen the firm could then mail to high value prospects. Did we also place them online? Sure. But that's not the reason for their creation. Their purpose was to share the results of a firm with some high value prospects, and not to 'improve SEO'. This firm would mail these out overnight to high value med mal, mesothelioma, traumatic injuries and other very serious injury victims. The thought was the video book would put this firm at the top of the list of potential firms these clients may be evaluating.

It's good to understand that producing a video in and of itself is a challenge. You have less than 10 seconds to gain their interest – and that's being overly generous. Even the most successful youtube artists spend weeks and months focusing on what works for them and their audience.

If you google "average watch time of a law firm video" – you will see a whole page filled with nothing BUT people who sell video production to firms.

The cost to produce a decent 2.5 minute video may range from $2,500-$5,000. How could you accurately measure your return on investment? The sad truth is that there are no REAL statistics currently available to measure the effectiveness in the law firm marketing world.

Before deciding to produce video content - consider what else YOU could do to market your firm for $5,000...

You could buy a firm profile on just about all three of the leading law firm directory sites and send SEO value and potential clients to your phones. With this you would also have trackable/measurable results.

An experienced law firm digital marketing agency could take that $5,000 ad budget and spend it on AdWords for Divorce, BK, DUI and alike and deliver YOU some serious clients.

As with any content being produced, make sure you have it's purpose in mind. Producing videos just to have one may not yield the results you expect. Make sure you know what you're going to do with that video, and how you'll take it to market first, then you may have a chance. Go forward with a purpose. If you are moving towards video creation, have fun doing it.

Podcasts - What Are They? Its Benefit to Businesses and Tips for Success

How would you define an audio podcast to someone who has never heard of them before? This question has often surfaced on various social media platforms, including Facebook. Interestingly, but perhaps not surprisingly, the answers varied quite a bit. Although the way people define what an audio podcast differs, the responses generally overlap in the following areas:

- Radio talk
- On-demand
- Free audio shows
- Niche

If you're not sure what a podcast is, we recommend you follow the link below (and then subscribe) to our own podcast. This will give you a great understanding of just what a podcast is PLUS ours will continue helping you along with your law firm's marketing.

https://anchor.fm/legalmarketing

What are Audio Podcasts?

We are not sure how many people are aware of this, but the word 'podcast' is actually a portmanteau of iPod and Broadcast.

Audio podcasting came into being as mostly an independent way for people to get their message out in the world and essentially build a community of individuals with mutual interests. But today podcasts have been adopted by several organizations, big and small, radio networks, comedians, TV networks, churches, storytellers and so much more.

There is not a predetermined or pre-planned length, style, production level, or any particular format of podcasts. They can be split into small episodes or seasons like what we see in a TV show or a serial.

Weekly releases of new episodes are standard, but podcasts can be released be daily, bi-weekly, or really any cadence the creator desires. In short, podcasts are generally a series of episodes.

These audio files or episodes are stored with a podcast hosting company. One of the best things about podcasts is that listeners can easily subscribe to podcast channels and get notified when the new episode comes out.

Podcasts are not only exciting, but they are also relatively very cheap and easy to produce, and anyone can benefit from the growing popularity of podcasts. You can talk about anything, or any topic that interests you and the best thing is you don't have to rely on the radio station for its recording and broadcasting.

4 Benefits of Podcasts for Attorneys

Law firms can use podcasts for multiple reasons, such as sharing information about a new service, talk about updates and/or new laws to practice areas, create brand awareness, generate more traffic, or foster relationships with the audience through engaging podcasts. Incorporating podcasts into the marketing strategy can provide several benefits to your law firm.

Fun Way to Drive Traffic

Podcasting can allow law firms to enhance their audience to reach efficiently and quickly. This can help the law firm to build familiarity with a wide range of listeners. Generally, people subscribe to a podcast channel, and the chances are that as long as the audio episodes keep coming out, the audience will quite likely listen to at least some of it.

In addition to this, podcasts can also help to drive referral traffic towards your law firm as many listeners recommend and share podcast channels with other people who share similar interests. Thus, this can significantly aid in the law firm's audience reach.

Foster Connection with The Listeners

Despite being a one-sided medium, podcasts are highly effective in building relationships and connections with the audience. The listeners often feel a close connection to the person speaking on the podcast as they listen to people that share a mutual interest or common notions.

This can allow law firms to build valuable relationships and foster trust; thus, listeners can be encouraged to associate themselves with the brand and lead to improved conversion rates as people are more likely to purchase something from a brand they know something about than a complete stranger.

Simple Way to Increase Brand Awareness

The consistency and familiarity of regular audio podcasts can help law firms to make their brand a household name. Law firms can integrate and relate the information about their services to the content of the podcast.

For instance, if you're a family law attorney, then produce a podcast about case law, new laws, common myths pertaining to divorce or child custody, etc. This way, podcasts can serve to be a medium of advertisement for your law firm.

Source of Additional Income
Connecting to the audience can help law firms to open more doors for the target audience to convert to clients.

SEO Benefits of a Podcast
As a form of content, you may be wondering just how podcasts can help you rank in the search engines - because it can. Here's how you can boost your SEO while living that podcast life.

Your podcast will likely focus around one or two topics. Try to select the most relevant of keywords pertaining to the topic, just like you would in blog writing. (Do you see where we're going with this?) Once you've identified your keywords, the next step is to write about each episode. Now, there are a few ways in which you can do this.

1. Transcription
2. Blog Writing
3. Hybrid

Transcription
Not quite a hybrid, a company called Rank Ranger regularly produces podcasts and is focused on transcription. In addition to writing regular blogs and content, they also have a podcast. In addition to the audio clip, they also provide a "here's what you can expect" overview, followed by a transcription of the entire podcast. This helps

them ensure they're content is not only getting out there but is helping their SEO and search engine rankings. Feel free to check out their blog section to get an understanding of what we're talking about:

https://www.bloomberg.com/podcasts/law

Blog Writing

If you were to go the route of writing a blog on the podcast episode, you'll want to ensure that you're employing SEO formatting with your heading tags, keywords, alt-text and meta descriptions. In addition to proper formatting, you should make sure your blog post has a minimum of 300 words, but preferably no lower than 500 words. This is a short but sweet recap of the podcast episode that can help your rank.

Hybrid

In the hybrid method, you're looking at writing a blog, but using quotes from the transcription to cut down on the amount of writing you'll need to do.

Bonus Tip: Maximize Your SEO Success with YouTube

Second only to Google, YouTube is the second most trafficked site out there with over 1 Billion users. Ensuring that your podcast makes it to your website for SEO and traffic purposes is great, but you can really maximize your success and exposure by also getting your podcast out there on YouTube. It is both free and easy to accomplish.

Check out our video podcast here: https://www.youtube.com/channel/UCCHTWLY8wtJaS8bRop8z88Q

Effective Podcast Tips for Success

There are a million reasons to get your podcast started today, and not a single reason not to. Having said that, there's a big difference between producing a podcast nobody listens to and producing a successful podcast that can help you with branding, marketing, and maybe even earn some big bucks.

Therefore, here are our top tips to produce and launch a successful podcast for your law firm.

Tip #1: Get Decent Equipment

The initial investment in equipment is relatively insignificant as compared to the probable gains. But that does not mean you have to spend thousands of dollars on cutting-edge equipment or software. Still, you should at least have a decent microphone, a headset, and some essential editing software to ensure your podcast sounds professional and clear.

Tip #2: Choose the Right Podcast Theme

The theme of a podcast can play a vital role in determining its success. Choose a theme that you not only care about but can also commit to for the long haul. If you're genuinely passionate about what you're speaking, it will resonate with other individuals who share the same thoughts. Being genuinely interested and informed in what you choose to talk about will keep the audience engaged and the listeners will appreciate you for it.

Tip #3: Find Balance

After launching your podcast, you'll probably start receiving suggestions and comments from the listeners. Some might want you to change the format, others might request for special guests; although it is always wise to listen to the needs of the audience, it is equally important to stay true to your identity. Therefore, be in control of the podcast and steer it in the direction that can spark real conversations rather than uninteresting content. Having said that, this does not mean that you completely ignore the wishes of the listeners. Find a balance between your podcast style and the recommendations or suggestions to successfully deliver content that is both loved by you and the audience.

Our podcasting equipment on a budget is here:

- USB Microphone Kit:

  https://www.amazon.com/gp/product/B07GQT8879

Going to be doing video podcasts? Here's our video equipment on a budget:

- Logitech BRIO:

  https://www.amazon.com/gp/product/B01N5NYRES

- Neewer LED Bi-Color Round Light:

  https://www.amazon.com/gp/product/B07WJJZKYJ

Infographics - What Are They? Benefits & Tips for Success

Surely nobody wants to spend a lot of time reading and trying to comprehend pages of intricate facts and figures. It is definitely not a coincidence that so much of the information that we share and see online today is in some form of pictorial representation.

There is a myriad of information surrounding us that is possibly not easy to grasp or remember in the limited amount of time that we have. However, using infographics is certainly an effective way to convey complex data and figures to readers and helps them to effectively understand and absorb information promptly.

But what are infographics? Why should your law firm be creating them?

Here we've brought you a complete guide to infographics to help you understand everything about this effective information displaying tool.

What Are Infographics?
Simply put, infographics are pictorial representations of information, knowledge, or data, specially designed to exhibit complex information clearly and quickly. Moreover, they're great for improving cognition by utilizing graphics to augment the human visual system's ability to see trends and patterns.

Infographics are all about telling a story; they help readers organize data and make complex information visually digestible so that way, readers can easily and quickly process the information. Infographics are used for numerous reasons; they are concise, entertaining, eye-catching, and useful.

Infographic Components
Infographics comprise of the following elements:

- **Content Elements:** include statistics, references, and time frames.
- **Visual Elements:** involve color, reference icons, and graphics.
- **Knowledge Elements:** involves facts and figures.

Why are Infographics Used?
Usually, infographics are used for a few of the following reasons:

Create Awareness
Create brand visibility and awareness or spread the word about a vital cause.

Illustrate Data
Present facts, statistics, and figures visually using graphs, charts, and other graphic tools.

Summarize Lengthy Content
Encapsulate lengthy blog posts, reports, and videos into a bite-sized visual representation.

Draw a Comparison
Visually compare two or more services, products, concepts, features, or brands.

Simplify Complex Information

Describe complex concepts with the help of visual illustrations and cues.

How Infographics Benefit Law Firms

Infographics are very beneficial for law firms, and it greatly helps to pass on essential information to target audiences in a fun and easy way. The following are a few of the many benefits of infographics received by law firms.

1. **Attractive and Engaging**
   Infographics are more engaging and fun as compared to plain text as they generally combine colors, images, content, and movement that naturally catches the eye. Post them to social media to create interest and engagement.

2. **Easy to View and Scan**
   Most people forget a lot of what they have read and tend to have short space attention spans, but they do remember what they've seen.

3. **Increased Traffic**
   Infographics are greatly sharable for use around the web. For instance, an infographic published in a WordPress blog or website usually issues an embed code. The code generates an automatic link from the original site to yours.

4. **Boost Brand Awareness**
   Infographics can be used to reinforce a brand, simply because they are visually appealing. Creating an infographic embedded with your logo and with your brand prominently displayed is a powerful means of increasing brand awareness.

5. **Search Engine Optimization**
   The viral nature of infographics makes people link to your site. Infographics can easily be shared on your Facebook, Twitter, Google+, LinkedIn, or Pinterest accounts, and it is there for all your followers to see.

Infographics are an entertaining, educational, and useful tool. They are an integral part of social media marketing and, more importantly, delivers vital information in a fun, engaging, and exciting way.

Infographic Tips for Success
Now that you know a little about infographics and the benefits it provides to law firms, here are few effective tips that can help you to take your visual graphics to the next level.

Tip #1: Foster Creativity and Originality
There are a plethora of visuals and infographics floating on the internet; so, if you want to get yours noticed, make sure to create something original and unique. Invest some time in research and discover what type of topics will most appeal to your target audience. Focus on questions that have been left unanswered and come up with creative ways to answer those questions.

If there is any topic that has already been covered earlier by someone else, but you still want to work on it, make sure you create an infographic with a new and fresh angle.

Tip #2: Know Your Audience
The most essential piece of homework one must do before building an infographic is to find out if it'll actually work with your target audience. Understand the type of topics

your audience will prefer and the designs that will appeal to them.

The most suitable tone of the content is also crucial to determine for your audience, as that tone will be used to craft a compelling copy of the infographic. Moreover, also figure out which social media platforms are mostly used by your target audience and create an infographic that performs best on those particular platforms.

Tip #3: Incorporate Attractive Fonts and Colors

Marketers all over the world rely on color psychology and, with its help, produce designs that deliver results. If your infographic does not use fonts and colors to bring your content to life and helps to resonate with the target audience, then it might fail to stand out among other infographics present on the web.

Tip #4: Less Text, More Visual Cues

Using a lot of text can make an infographic seem uninteresting and boring. Therefore, ensure you use a lot of visual cues and a limited amount of text. One way to do this is to supplement or replace labels, subheadings, captions, and other text present in the infographic with images, illustrations, or icons.

Tip #5: Create a Visual Hierarchy

Establishing a visual hierarchy is all about arranging and organizing information on the infographic according to the order or level of importance. That way, viewers can easily scan through from one section to another. Incorporating visual hierarchy can make your infographic look attractive, professional, and cleaner.

Infographics are an excellent way to share complex information in a concise, attractive, and easy to understand way. They are gaining popularity with each passing day, and several businesses have tried to incorporate this tool in their content marketing strategies; some have flourished while others have not. If you want your name to be among the successful, make sure to follow the 'infographic tips for success' shared earlier.

There are a ton of free infographic design tools out there. Our favorite is canva.com. In fact, we use this for a lot of graphic creation.

Social Media and Content Marketing

All right so social media is its own brand of marketing. However, social media marketing does intersect with content marketing as the posts that you're creating and pushing out on your social networks are a form of content. While they both may intersect, it is important to remember that they are in fact two very different entities.

Differences Between Social Media Marketing and Content Marketing

There are three primary differences between social media marketing and content marketing. Those differences are their operations, the content, and their objectives. Let's take a closer look.

Operations

Social media marketing is conducted on the social platforms themselves, such as Facebook, Instagram, Twitter, etc. Content marketing is normally (though not always) centered around your law firm's website (i.e. blogs, infographics, eBooks, etc.). Social media is a great way to maximize the exposure of your website's content though.

Let's take a blog for example. Many law firms are blogging these days to help drive traffic, provide value and to ensure they're continuing to hit on those SEO keywords to rank higher. How do you get people to read your blog? Well, you could post about it on social media and hope that people click on the link to read your article. You could also pay to boost that post on social media, displaying it to an even larger audience. What's important to keep in mind here is that the content itself is on your website and social media is a means of gaining exposure and is simply housing the link back to your website.

Content

Each social media platform has their own unique nuances when it comes to posting. Twitter, for instance, you can post up to 140 characters per post and you can include hashtags in your post to help reach a larger audience *organically*. Instagram is primarily focused on photos, but they do give you a place to include your post and again, uses hashtags to reach a wider audience with your messaging.

As the content is housed on your own website in content marketing, you have the ability to house larger content - such as blog posts.

Objectives

The two main objectives behind social media marketing are brand awareness and customer satisfaction. You want people to be exposed to your brand in order to bring in some new business. Additionally, you want to keep your customers happy and your social media pages provide them with value-driven content and a direct line of communication. It provides current and prospective clients with a way to ask questions and develop brand loyalty.

Content marketing is more focused around demand generation. You want to spark interest in what you have to offer and as they visit your website, you can begin to develop a relationship with them and nurture them towards lead conversion.

What is Demand Generation?

Demand generation is exactly what it says - a generation of demand for a law firms' services. It's a way for marketing and sales to work together to nurture prospective clients. It is a way of getting people <u>interested</u> in your services and is not to be confused with lead generation, which is the task of turning interest into sales.

The Intersection

Now, you may be wondering with so many major differences between the two, at what point do they intersect? Great question. The *content* itself is where social media marketing and content marketing meet. What are you posting to social media? Pictures, updates, blog links, videos, infographics, etc. Those are all examples of content and a part of content marketing.

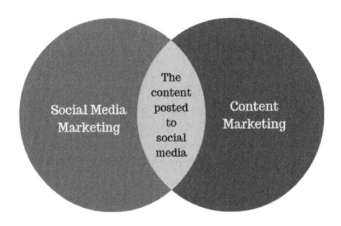

Aligning Your Strategies

Getting your content blasted out on social media is fundamental to building your brand awareness and reaching large audiences. When your social media and content marketing strategies are aligned, you've positioned yourself for a higher ROI. Some benefits of an aligned strategy include:

- Builds brand awareness
- Relevant and value driven content to current and potential customers
- Influences prospects
- Attract potential customers
- Drives traffic to your website or landing page
- Return at every stage of the sales funnel
- Client retention
- Customer satisfaction

With social media, you're able to meet potential customers before they are even in the market for your service. One in three people were active on social media networks in the last year, making social media crucial to your brand's online success.

Conducting Research

Who is your target audience? What common interests do they have? What keywords are they using to find your law firm and your competitors in your practice areas on the search engine? What questions are they asking? Understanding the answer to those questions can help shape your content marketing strategy and determine which platforms your law firm should be marketing on (*see our chapter on platforms*). Unless you're running paid advertisements, social media accounts are free to create and maintain. So, what have you got to lose?

Establish KPIs to Measure Your Success

What Are KPIs?
KPIs stands for Key Performance Indicators and they are a set of quantifiable measurements used to gauge a performance.

Measuring Success
When aligning your social media and content marketing you're looking to build awareness for your brand, drive traffic to your website, boost engagement for your page and increase conversions. How do you measure the success of each of those to know whether your strategy is working or if you need to shift focus? Through your KPIs.

Awareness

The two key metrics you can use to measure whether you've been successful in building brand awareness through your social media efforts are through the number of impressions and the number of people reached.

Impressions are the total number of times people have seen the content. Reach is the total number of unique profiles that your content has been shown to. You see, one person may have seen your content three or four times. Meaning chances are pretty good that your reach will be much lower than your impressions.

Drive Traffic
When looking to measure the success of this goal, some KPIs you'll want to consider are website clicks. This tells you how many people have clicked on the link to your website from the post. If you've got your Facebook Pixel installed correctly, all of those people will have been caught in your Pixel's web so you can retarget to them later on.

Boost Engagement

Engagement is measured through things like "likes", comments, shares, pageviews, social mentions, followers and sessions. No one KPI will tell the whole story. They are all unique pieces of a puzzle and when put together can give you a more accurate visual of whether you've been successful in boosting engagement.

Increase Conversions

The money maker and goal we're all trying to accomplish - increasing conversions. This success of this stage will be determined by your website. You can use Google Analytics (if you have the code installed on your website) to help you track who was on what page, how long did they spend and what page did they visit next. While aligning your social media and content marketing strategies, did you notice an increase in blog subscribers? Increased traffic to your service pages?

Using Insights to Provide Insight

See what we did there? Yup, this author is a total nerd.

Each social media platform typically has a version of analytics that you can use to help gauge some of those KPIs without having to dig very far.

- Facebook Insights
- Instagram Insights
- LinkedIn Analytics
- Twitter Audience Insights

Each of those platforms offer a bird's eye view of KPIs. *This is only available for company pages and not for individual profiles.*

Measuring the KPIs isn't as difficult as it probably sounds and if you're going to do something, isn't it worth it to do it right the first time?

Determine Your Strategy

Your strategy for aligning your social media and content marketing can help improve your ROI and maximize your law firm's effectiveness.

Audit Your Current Social Media Pages

Before you get started, you really need to do a run through of your law firm's current social media pages. Here are some things you'll want to keep an eye out for:

- What social platforms is your law firm on?
- Are there any duplicate pages?
- Is the information on your pages accurate and up to date?
- Are all of the fields filled out in their entirety?
- Are your pages all uniform? (i.e. they all look the same to promote brand awareness/brand recognition)
- Remove any inactive accounts.
- Ensure the social links on your website are 1) there and 2) correct.

Ensuring your pages are optimized before you start working on boosting engagement can help you put your best foot forward. An inaccurate or incomplete page may give the impression that you're lazy or unprofessional. Yes, it is that serious.

Define Your Target Audience

We talked about this briefly a bit earlier in this chapter. Based on who your target audience is, what type of content should you be producing? How will you capture their attention? What social platforms are your target audience using? Those are the platforms that you want to be on as well. For instance, if your target audience is primarily using Facebook, then that should be your primary focus when it comes to social media.

Establish Brand Personality, Tone and Voice

Understanding *who* you are marketing to, can help you shape *how* you talk to them (i.e. brand personality, tone and voice). An older generation may not be up on the latest hip new slang whereas the younger demographic might be. Identifying the right tone can help you maintain a consistent message across the various platforms.

When companies make the decision to rebrand, this may also mean rebranding their tone. An awesome example of this is Wendy's. They went from meh to a HUGE following in Twitter with awesome Tweets that will have you rolling on the floor with laughter. Seriously, go check out Wendy's on Twitter - you won't regret it.

Research the Competitive Landscape

Scope out your competitor's social media accounts. What platforms are they using? How many times a week are they posting? What kind of content are they posting? Is it working? Knowing this can help you determine what *is* working and what's *not* working for them so you can take the best and the worst to help shape your own strategy.

Build a Social Media Content Calendar

Arguably, this may be the most fundamental step in a successful social media strategy. It helps you plan ahead, stay organized, maximizes efficiency and leads content creation.

Conduct Periodic Reviews

Just because you've checked all of the boxes doesn't mean you're done. People change. The economy changes - some years more than others (*cough* 2020 *cough*). By conducting periodic reviews you're able to identify if anything needs to be changed to meet the new demands. There will come a time in the not so distant future that you'll need to adjust your strategy. It's like shampoo bottles say - lather, rinse, repeat. Only in this case, it's audit, define, establish, research, calendar, repeat.

Part 5:

Social Media

Social Media Marketing for Lawyers

As an individual, you might think of social media as a place to socialize and blow off steam, or maybe chat with friends, and post pictures of your latest vacation. However, for law firms, it can be so much more than that. Social media is an important chance to not only reach out to potential clients, but also brand yourself as a recognizable and helpful go-to source in the legal industry.

Social media marketing is one piece of a multi-faceted digital marketing strategy that can help you with branding your law firm and gaining exposure. The best part? It's free.

Every mention of your brand is a chance to not only gain publicity for your services, but on social media, it's your chance to control the direction of the conversation. It allows you to thoughtfully guide your story.

Whether you rely on LinkedIn, Facebook, Twitter or Instagram, how you present your law firm helps you create the vision of who you are and what you represent.

One of the most important elements to marketing your law firm on social media is determining where your target audience is. What we're saying here is that if you're a divorce lawyer and you know that statistically, the younger demographic (20's) has a higher divorce rate, you may want to consider social media marketing on Instagram. However, Facebook's users are made up of approximately 70% of the U.S. adult population, meaning this is a great platform to advertise on to reach the wider audience. It helps that Facebook also owns Instagram as well. However, we're going to cut this topic short here as we'll delve into what social platforms your law firm should be using here shortly.

Tips for Social Media Success

Here are some tips to help you make the most out of your law firm's social media presence:

- Keep a consistent look to your content by using branded colors or similar pictures and logos so you easily become recognizable regardless of which site a client finds you on.
- Business descriptions and about sections should be consistent across the board, again pointing to brand recognition like we mentioned above with a logo or your company colors.
- When using photos of either you or the other attorneys/employees at your law firm, ensure that it looks professional. It presents you in a manner that promotes confidence in future clients and customers.
- Include quality content that matches your industry, in this case, the legal industry. This is not the place to discuss the fishing rally you went to last weekend. Stay on-point, on-message, and show people why you're a trusted authority in your practice area(s).
- Don't forget to be human. Participating in a charity event? Celebrating a work anniversary or a birthday? Your followers/potential clients want to see your human side, which can help make the emotional connection with your law firm.

How Social Media Can Help Your Law Firm Grow

Think about these businesses for a moment: McDonald's, Coca-Cola, and Verizon.

Almost instantly, an opinion was formed. You probably imagined their logo or thought of their slogans. Did you think of one of their commercials? The point is that you immediately knew who they were and what they represented. You knew what their brand colors were.

It's because of consistency, seeing the same things over and over, that subconsciously we connect to a brand. Even in a nanosecond, when you heard the name McDonald's, your brain was already forming a thought around them. This is what brand consistency does.

Sure, they are massive global brands with massive ad campaigns, but you can replicate the same thing for your law firm. By using those same tactics and strategies, you can create brand recognition in your law firm.

When clients are exposed to you on multiple occasions, each time you touch them through your marketing they're slowly layering those thoughts and images. By keeping them consistent, you're doing what those mega-companies are doing. You're solidifying your brand in a way that they'll remember, all from the repeated exposure.

Why Images Matter...

A professional image instills confidence. If you showed up to a doctor appointment, and your doctor was dressed as if he'd just got back from a camping trip or was fly-fishing in waders, you might have hesitations. The truth is, as much as we want to believe it shouldn't matter, if you don't present yourself in a professional way, people lose confidence - particularly when it comes to lawyers.

Use Well-Positioned Content to Build Authority

Use a consistent voice and tone across your social media channels. Just as you want a consistent appearance, you need to keep a similar voice. It shows customers you not only know what you're talking about, but that you're an authority on the topic.

When you build trust, it helps form relationships. This is how a client chooses a law firm to represent them. They want to know they're in good hands, and your ability to share your knowledge is a perfect opportunity to showcase your skills.

With each of these ideas, you can build a presence that is not only recognized, but also respected. Why wouldn't you want to take advantage of that opportunity? Make sure you have a well-represented brand across social media today, as this is a vital element of your digital marketing strategy.

What Social Platforms Should Your Law Firm Be Using and Why

There are plenty of new and trendy social media platforms popping up all the time. How do determine which platforms your law firm should be marketing on? The answer comes down to this: What social platforms is your target audience using? Those are the platforms your law firm should be conducting social media marketing on.

Let's take a look at the top five social media platforms and the various demographics to help you figure out which ones are more valuable to your law firm. Bear in mind that all of these platforms are free to maintain a business page on and there's no reason why your law firm couldn't post to *all* of them.

Target Audience
Understanding who your target audience is can really help you succeed in social media marketing. For instance, one study showed that the divorce rate was highest between the ages of 20 to 24 for both men and women. Knowing that and further refining your target audience can help you understand which platforms would be your best option for targeting them on social media. Which platforms is that demographic using?

Facebook

With over 2.41 billion monthly active users, Facebook is the largest of all social networks. If there was one platform to rule them all, Facebook would be it. Did you get our Lord of the Rings reference? (Proud nerd here!) When it comes to *global* visibility, Facebook is only outranked by Google and YouTube.

Out of the 2.41 billion monthly active users, 10% of them are Americans (approximately 241 million). Of those 241 million, approximately 71% of those American users are adults. That's 171+ million American adult users of the platform and 171+ million potential clients out there.

Let's break down Facebook users by demographic:

75% of women use Facebook and 63% of men use it. While there is a slight disparity amongst genders, there is a much wider disparity amongst age. Take a look:

- 18 - 24: 76%
- 25 - 29: 84%
- 30 - 49: 79%
- 50 - 64: 68%
- 65+: 46%

While the numbers may be lower for older adults, seniors are the fastest growing group of Facebook users. eMarketer predicts Facebook will see a 7% growth in the 65+ age bracket.

Looking to target those who are a bit wealthier? Facebook averages that about 74% of high-income earners maintain profiles on the platform.

It's undeniable that Facebook is *the* platform to market on regardless of industry. Should your law firm maintain a business page on Facebook? Absolutely. Without question.

LinkedIn

Ranked as the fifth most popular social media platform, there are approximately 675 million monthly active users with 167 million of them being Americans. That's approximately 27% of Americans. Breaking down the demographics again, 57% of LinkedIn users are men with the remaining 43% being female.

Here's another eye-opening number for you: 61% of LinkedIn users are between the ages of 25 to 34 years old.

While it may seem a platform employment lawyers would thrive on, it's not just for employment lawyers. If your demographic lines up with those using this platform, then you should absolutely consider maintaining a business page on it.

Twitter

There are roughly 330 million monthly active users on Twitter with about 145 million logging in daily. Of those 145 million, approximately 30 million daily users are American. Going back to the highest rate of divorce per age bracket, remember the bracket was 20 to 24 years old. A whopping 44% of American daily users are between the ages of 18 - 24.

While there are naysayers out there who don't believe marketing their law firm on Twitter will make a difference, it all comes down to *who* you're marketing to and which strategies you're employing. There are quite a number of law firms who have found success on Twitter.

Instagram

Another platform that some attorneys don't see value in. This platform is a visual one, centered around photos.

While users have the ability to write a caption with the photo, the photo should be good enough to stand alone to get the point across as the caption is not the focal point of the post. However, couple that with the ability to use hashtags to reach a wider audience organically and you're in for a treat.

I digress. Let's get back to the numbers. There are approximately 1 billion monthly active users on Instagram with 110 million being located in the United States. That brings us to approximately 37% of American adults using the social platform. Instagram is by far more popular among younger demographics with 67% of users being between ages 18 - 29. 62% of users say they have become more interested in a brand or product after seeing it in Stories.

Social Media: What Should Your Law Firm Be Posting

Once you've determined who your target audience is and what social networking platforms are the best to reach your audience on, the next logical question would be - what should your law firm be posting?

What Should You Be Posting on Social Media?

Great question and we're glad you asked it. Are you posting blogs to your website? Those are great to publish to social media as they provide relevant and value-driven information and also, drive traffic to your website.

Are there any law updates pertaining to your practice areas? Keep your current and potential clients informed of any new legislation. Has your law firm been featured in any new articles, interviews or even podcasts? Those are also great to push out to your social media pages.

What's going on in the news pertaining to your practice areas? Links to relevant articles are great to post. Your law firm likely gets some frequently asked questions, consider answering some of those frequently asked questions on your social media pages. You could either make a simple post, graphic or even answer the question by going Live on Facebook or other social platforms.

Looking for some ideas to bolster engagement? How about a joke?! Let's face it, there are many legal jokes out there and showing your humorous side can also show your human side and can help you build a connection.

In our experience we've found the most engaging posts to be those of a more personal nature. Not that you should dive into your personal life, but rather posts about promotions, birthdays, meet the team, etc. Your current and potential customers want to relate to you and celebrate with you. That human connection is important to securing their trust and confidence.

How Often Should I Be Posting?

Precision Legal Marketing recommends between 3 - 5 posts per week, though that isn't set in stone. The number of posts your law firm should be making really depends on your goals. If you're just trying to stay relevant and active, then 2 - 3 posts per week is plenty. If your law firm is trying to dominate social media and get ahead of the game with both paid and organic strategies, 3 - 5 posts per week is great.

The answer may vary based on your goals, but if you're really not sure still, why not test it? Spend 30 days posting 2 - 3 times per week and the following 30 days posting between 3 - 5 times per week. After the 60 days go back and look at whether you saw an increase in engagements, followers, traffic, etc. If not, posting 2 - 3 times per week is probably fine for your law firm.

Why Is My Post Reach So Low?

Unless you're paying for advertising, your social posts aren't going to be shown to your entire audience of followers. Let's look at Facebook to answer this question as it is the primary platform for the majority.

You have 100 followers on your law firm's Facebook business page. Yet when you post some valuable content to your page your metrics show that you've only reached 20 people with only one or two engagements. So, why aren't your posts reaching a larger audience? Facebook will only show your business page's post to a small group of people. If people engage with your post it demonstrates that your post is relevant and so, Facebook will show it to another group of people. The more people engage with your posts, the more people your posts will be shown to and the more people you'll reach.

Thanks to Facebook's algorithm updates in recent years, your social posts are only going to reach about 1.6% - 2% of your followers - give or take a few depending on the level of engagement. This means that if you have 100 followers you can expect your post to reach 16 - 20 people without any engagement. Those numbers are the reason why you need to be creating relevant, value-driven and engaging content, to build your following and reach a wider audience organically.

Of course, if you pay to boost the post or to run any advertisements this can help you gain more exposure for your posts, page and law firm as well.

What Should Your Law Firm NOT Be Posting?

Just as important as what you should be posting is what you should NOT be posting. Knowing that without engagement your posts aren't reaching many people it may be tempting to post off topic stuff like beauty trends or car hacks. They might be great for boosting engagement, but it's the wrong engagement.

When you look to run advertisements on Facebook or social media, they give you the option to target your followers and those who interact with your page. If those engaging with your page are doing so because you are posting stuff unrelated to your practice areas, they are not likely to convert to clients. At the end of the day, that's what social media marketing is all about - lead generation and bringing in new clients. There's limited to no Return on Investment (ROI) on targeting the wrong audience.

Optimizing Your Law Firm's Social Presence

As we've already covered the basics of *why* social media and *how* it fits into the content marketing equation, let's look at some best practices and ways of optimizing your law firm's presence.

Social Media Best Practices

As with everything, there are some best practices to be mindful of when establishing your presence on social media.

DO remain consistent across the platforms. Many law firms choose to create business profiles on a variety of platforms such as Facebook, LinkedIn, Twitter and Instagram. Your profile picture, cover photo, description, contact details, etc. should all be exactly the same across each platform. This can help create brand recognition and brand awareness as well as demonstrating quality and professionalism.

DO complete your profiles. Don't skimp on the details or leave anything blank. Provide as much information as you can to ensure your audience has enough to make an informed decision.

DO post regularly. Posting to your social accounts 2 - 3 times per week is a great number. Anything more than that may be seen as excessive and could result in your law firm's page being "unliked" or "unfollowed". Although, the number of posts per week is a general guideline and not a rule. Conduct competitor research to see what's working for them and what's not to help you figure out how often you should be posting.

DO hashtag research. Obscure hashtags that aren't used by many people will fall on deaf ears, meaning no one will see your post. In the search bar of LinkedIn, Twitter and Instagram you have the ability to search for hashtags and the results will tell you how many posts have been made with them. The more that's posted to it, the more views that content is getting. For instance, #divorce has a *big* following but #yourlawfirmsname will likely have almost no results.

DO provide relevant and timely information. Use this as a way to spread news on your practice areas. If your law firm's primary practice area is personal injury and we just hit the summer months, posting about motorcycle accidents and dog bites, things that people are looking for right now, can be a great way to drive engagement. (Google Trends can help you find season trends like the one in the example.)

DON'T be disappointed with low organic reach. Only 1.6 to 2 percent of your followers will see your organic posts. A great way to boost these numbers is by getting people to engage with your posts. The more that engage, the more the post will be shown to.

DON'T post irrelevant content. Your law firm's social media page shouldn't post on things such as Hollywood drama (unless you practice family law and you're discussing the latest "it" couple's divorce) or fashion. They may be a great way of getting engagement, but you're attracting people who are *not* likely to convert to clients thereby defeating the purpose of social media marketing.

Consider Advertising

A great way to expand your reach *and* to draw in new, qualified leads for your law firm is through advertising on social media. Facebook, for instance, allows you to create forms that potential clients can fill out with their information. Those results then populate in an Excel form that you can download and provide to your receptionist to reach out to.

Social Media Advertising can also help you build up your followers and drive engagement. For law firms just starting out on social media, this may be a great way to build your following.

Optimizing Your Facebook Business Page

There are six basic steps to optimizing your firm's business page on Facebook and they are:

1. Select the right type of page
2. Custom username
3. Images
4. Fill out all of your details - Don't leave any blanks!
5. Ensure your contact information is accurate
6. Remove/hide unused tabs

Let's walk through those six steps.

Select the Right Type of Page

When you first create your Facebook business page, you'll be able to choose from a variety of options such as:

- Local business or place
- Company
- Brand or Product

- Public Figure
- Entertainment
- Cause or Community

By selecting the right type of page from the onset it can help enhance the way you communicate the message your law firm wishes to show.

Create a Custom Username

You have the ability to create your own username. For instance, on Facebook the Precision Legal Marketing username is @precisionlegalmarketing. However, if you'd like something different or want it to match other social accounts who don't offer the ability to be choosy, you do have some flexibility there. We've noticed in some cases that those who don't create a username for their page just don't end up with one at all. So, make sure that you've checked the box and create a custom username for your business page, so you don't end up with a random string of alpha-numeric characters for your Facebook slug.

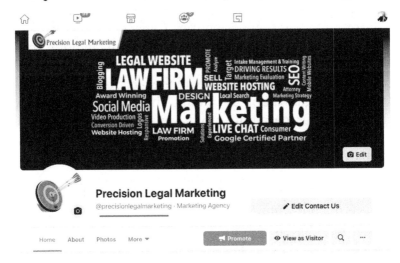

Images

All right. Now, what picture should you post for your law firm? The local courthouse? The managing partners? A group/staff photo? Logo? While the answer may differ depending on your brand and practice area(s), the majority of law firms favor using their logo. This can really help you create brand awareness and brand recognition for your firm. The trick to your profile and cover image is consistency. Again, in an effort to foster brand recognition and brand awareness you want to present a consistent brand across your digital marketing efforts such as social media platforms and on your website.

Fill Out All Your Details - Don't Leave Any Blanks!

All right. This is one of the most common issues we run

across when we take over the social media marketing for our clients. Either missing or inaccurate information throughout their business page. Ensure that you input as much as you can into your profile such as your contact information, set your categories (what industry are you in?), your about section, "our story" and even your open hours. Not only does this help users find you easier, but it also helps to instill confidence in the fact that you're a professional organization not taking a half-hearted approach. Incomplete or inaccurate profiles may be a negative sign to potential buyers, indicating that your cut corners (though not always).

Ensure Your Contact Information is Accurate

This is not only important so that your potential customers can find you, but also for local SEO purposes. Counting as a directory listing (aka citation) you want to ensure you have accurate information to promote your local SEO and to avoid being down ranked. If Google or the other search engines aren't clear on your correct contact information so as to provide accurate information to their users, they may end up downranking your website.

Remove/Hide Unused Tabs

While you won't have the ability to turn off *all* of the tabs, you do have the ability to turn off a bunch of them. If they're not relevant and/or you're not using them, turn them off so they don't appear on your business page. Just one step closer to having that spiffy, professional page that demonstrates your brand's level of quality.

Linking Instagram to Your Facebook Page

Now owned by Facebook, Instagram is yet another free social networking site for you to capitalize on. You have the ability to simultaneously post to both Facebook and Instagram by linking your accounts. You can accomplish this by clicking on Settings from your Facebook Business Page and then clicking on Instagram on the left side menu.

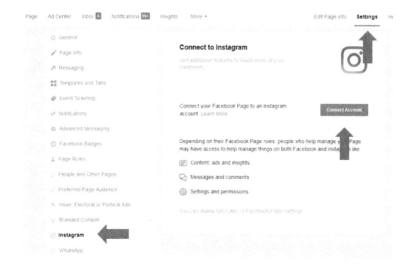

Once you've clicked on the Instagram tab, click on the blue button labeled "Connect Account". During this process you'll be asked to provide your username and password to login to your Instagram account in order to establish the connection. You may also be asked to upgrade to a business account as many people sign-up initially as individuals and not businesses. That's it. It's really just that simple.

Optimizing Other Pages

Once you've completed your business page and all of your information is accurate and filled in, you can then move on to optimizing your other profiles as well. Not to say that you *have* to start with your Facebook account, but whatever account you choose to start with, make sure that the information you put out there is all consistent across all profiles, pages and accounts.

Social Media Advertising

Social media networks, like Facebook, give you the ability to advertise to expand your reach into new pools of individuals. If you're creating content such as kick butt blogs, you'll want to make sure you're driving traffic as best you can to those blogs. Advertising on social media is a great way to do that. In addition to helping you build brand awareness and drive traffic to your website, you're also able to conduct lead generation through having individuals fill out forms to qualify them, taking your marketing and lead generation efforts to the next level. Bear in mind that social media advertising is so much more than just boosting a post.

Facebook Live
Best Practices for Lawyers

These days, video is everything and Facebook Live counts as video. It may not be pre recorded, but it is a *great* way to reach your followers and get them to tune into what you're saying. As with all forms of content, remember that your Facebook Live should provide value to your followers in hopes that you'll convert them to clients - a great tool for social media marketing for lawyers.

What is Facebook Live?

Facebook Live is a feature on the social network, Facebook, that allows users to record themselves *live* (aka real-time and not prerecorded). Users have the ability to determine who can see their video. It is a great way of boosting engagements and connecting directly with your audience.

All you need is a camera and a Facebook profile or page.

If you're wanting to go live in an effort to boost your law firm's brand awareness and maybe even generate a few leads, you'll want to go live directly from your page and not your own personal profile. Did you know that you're able to go live on Facebook connected through your Zoom?! That's right, Facebook live just made things a bit more user friendly.

According to HubSpot, as of 2018 there were over 78% of online audiences watching video on Facebook Live.

Those watching your Facebook Live video will be able to like and comment on the feed, giving you direct access to them. Law firms who choose to go Live often end up answering various questions posed by those watching the video. They would simply post a question in the comments that you're able to see and answer *Live*.

8 Facebook Live Best Practices

1. As with everything, there are some best practices to going Live on Facebook.

2. Always test out your live video before sharing your live feed with your followers. You're able to do this by changing the video to "only me" in the privacy settings in Facebook's live section.

3. Space out your Facebook Live from other posts. Facebook typically shows traditional posts to about 1.6 - 2% of your followers, depending on the level of engagement. With Facebook Live, however, Facebook will rank Live higher than traditional posts, giving you a wider organic reach to your feed. Spacing out your content can help you achieve a higher level of organic reach.

4. Keep reintroducing yourself. When you turn on your Facebook Live feed it may take your followers a minute or so to tune in to your video. This is why it's important to every so often pause and reintroduce yourself. A quick "For those just tuning in..." comment here and there during your video can really help out!

5. Encourage viewers to Like and share the video. Going back to the engagement statistic, the more

people who interact with your post (like, share, comment), the more people that will see your post (and hopefully engage). You can get creative in how you ask your viewers to share your video. For instance:

Engage your audience in "non-law" banter. This will help you be less stiff and more relaxed. Things like: "Thumbs up if you like the X hockey team." Or even "Share this with someone you think is strong and capable." (or another descriptor for those that may fall in your target audience).

6. Engage with viewers who are commenting on your video and call them out by first name only. Your audience will be thrilled to hear you mentioning their name, and even more delighted that you're taking the time to address their questions or concerns, thus providing value to them. Another plus to this is that Facebook's algorithm will assign your video a higher relevancy score the more comments your video has, meaning it will show up on more people's News Feeds.

7. Broadcast for at least 10 minutes. As soon as your Facebook Live starts recording, you'll slowly start appearing in your follower's News Feeds. It may take them a few minutes to get their video fired up. Going Live for at least 10 minutes (though you can stay live for up to 90 minutes) give everyone time to tune in and to have plenty of time to ask questions, leave comments and ultimately, engage with your video.

8. Take a bow and thank your audience. Well, maybe not an actual bow, but you should sign off with a closing such as "Thanks for watching" or "I'll be

going live again soon." You could even make the call to action once more for both your business and for your viewers to like and share the video.

My biggest piece of advice is to have fun with this. Grab someone else in the firm and do it together. Tell stories and share information about interesting cases you have been involved with or interested in yourself. This isn't for everyone, but give it a try and see if you don't get a client from it. I dare you.

Part 6:

Advertising

Why You Should Be Advertising for Your Law Firm In The First Place?

Now, there are several ways in which to advertise your law firm. First, let's talk about what advertising is so you get a good feel for it before diving in. In some circles in the legal community, it's a dirty word. It really isn't. As a business owner, it's essential, and just because you have a law degree doesn't mean you shouldn't be a business owner first.

Advertising is a form of *paid* marketing in which law firms can have their content displayed before a larger audience. The key word here is *paid.*

At this point, we've already talked a little bit about the difference between paid and organic, but for a quick recap: organic is where our content is awesome and it naturally attracts people to it (usually through SEO) whereas paid/ advertising is where we're paying to have our content displayed to people who would not necessarily otherwise know we exist.

While there are many forms of paid advertising like TV, Radio, Print and Digital, we are focussing on digital in these pages. There are essentially three main primary forms of digital advertising that can benefit your law firm are PPC, PPL and Social Advertising. There are other niche forms, but let's take a closer look at the more traditional forms.

What are the main current forms of advertising?

PPL (Pay Per Lead)

Let's knock this out early. Pay Per Lead is where you only pay when you get a valid lead instead of a view or click. It's basically buying leads online yourself or from other sources such as Nolo.com, Lawyers.com or FindLaw. They use various marketing efforts to drive leads to websites and capture intake that they then turn around and resell to you. Often this intake gets sent to multiple firms at the same time. So with this type of marketing, it's crucial you make first contact. These leads can be very effective and are often in my toolbox for a new firm hanging a shingle. I mentioned you can also bring leads in yourself that are considered PPL. Google's newly launched LSA (Local Service Ads) are another form of this type of lead generation. Google now has ads running across the top (on top of the PPC ads themselves) of the search results that feature attorneys as being "Google Screened".

The above image shows where the Google Local Service Ads are located. While these are run by Google, they are billed as pay per lead meaning, you pay when you get a valid lead and not by click. These have only been offered for a few months in many markets across the country but are proving to shake up the landscape when it comes to marketing on Google in general.

PPC (Pay Per Click)

Now we'll take a look at PPC (*Pay Per Click*). PPC means that you'll get charged for when people click on your advertisement. Hence the term *pay per click*. I'm about to nerd out on you guys, so bear with me....

As we covered a few minutes ago, there are two ways to rank on Google (and the other search engines), either organically or via ads.

We talked about the importance of SEO and how it can

help you rank higher earlier in this book. However, if your SEO isn't quite on point yet (it can take 4 - 6 months minimum to start seeing improvement in many cases), you're likely not ranking very well in the search engines.

The best place to hide a dead body is page 2 of Google's Search results....

If you're ranking on page one, you're likely getting your market share of traffic to your website. And more traffic means more potential clients. This is why SEO is so important.

But what if your SEO isn't where it needs to be and you're not ranking very well?

That's where PPC comes in.

The most common form of PPC is Google Ads. Let's pause here for a second...

Chances are likely that you've queried Google for something in the past. Let's say we wanted to look for a divorce lawyer in Virginia Beach. So, we plug our search term into Google and hit enter. Here's what we see:

Before we get to any search results who are appearing *organically* through SEO efforts, we can see this advertisement. This right here is a Google Ads ad - a PPC ad. This firm has paid Google for the top spot on your search feed for those keywords.

So, using Google's Ads, you now have the ability to rank on page one while you continue to work on your SEO efforts. You'd have to be blind not to see the benefit there. A word of caution though, when you're not familiar with Google Ads, you may not see the cost benefit there as your ROI may be lower. You see, just like in SEO, you're looking for long-tail keywords with a low competition score as they'll have a lower PPC cost.

Let's move on to social media advertising.

Social Media Advertising

Your page may have a decent size following, but if they're not engaging with your page and your posts, there's a pretty good chance that your content won't show on their timeline. The more a person interacts with your posts, and page as a whole, the more Facebook will show your content. How can you get around this? Through paid advertisements.

Facebook Ads allow you to create advertisements aimed at your target audience. Not just your followers, but all of those who can fit in your target audience demographics (depending on your budget). We've seen some pretty awesome results come from advertising on Facebook. And the best part is that when you choose to advertise on Facebook, you also have the ability to advertise simultaneously on Instagram and Facebook's Audience Network which is composed of thousands of partners, including some popular apps. It allows you to reach your audience wherever they might be to so that you can more effectively get your message out there.

Are Facebook Ads for Lawyers?

Facebook is the reigning king of social media. It has more than 2.41 billion monthly active users around the world. In addition, 68% of Americans use the site, and 74% of users log on daily. The platform is growing year over year, and doesn't show signs of slowing down anytime soon. If you want to advertise on a social media site that's going to cast as wide a net as possible, Facebook is your place.

Many lawyers have found Facebook highly useful when it comes to generating leads for their firms. They can find new clients and increase their profits simply by posting the right kind of ads and gearing them towards the right audiences. However, the lawyers that have been successful also know which advertising tools and best practices to employ to ensure their campaigns will make the most impact.

If you're going to use Facebook advertising for your law firm, here are some best practices to keep in mind. This is not meant to be a technical tutorial but rather a starting point for best practices. We also wanted to cover some topics we haven't seen covered. You may want to join the facebook group *Facebook Ads for Beginners*, too:

https://www.facebook.com/groups/
FBAdvertisingForBeginners

Connect the Facebook Pixel to Your Website NOW – even if you aren't running ads

The Facebook pixel is a piece of code that you add to every page of your website. When a lead takes some sort of action, like signs up for an email list or requests information through a form, the Facebook Pixel kicks into gear and reports it. You can track leads who went to your website after they saw your Facebook ad, and begin to build custom audiences that will be likely to convert after seeing your ad.

The pixel also works in the reverse. Let's say someone stumbled across your firm's website on Google, searched around for information and then logged onto Facebook. They would then start to see your firm's ads on their newsfeed.

So, for example, perhaps late one night, a woman is sitting on her computer, searching for divorce lawyers after having a fight with her husband. She is not ready to divorce yet, but she wants to find out about the process. She goes to your site, spends a few minutes on it and gets the information she needs. When she is ready to file for divorce a few months down the line, she will remember your firm, because she's seeing your ads on her Facebook feed.

Without the Facebook pixel, you don't know who your audience is or who converted, so it's useless to try and run a campaign. You need data on your website visitors in order to be truly effective with Facebook advertising. The longer you have a pixel installed, the larger your audience can grow. So, install a pixel as soon as you can and connect to an ad account.

Think About Using Lead Ads Instead of Regular Ads or Boosted Content

Lead ads for Facebook can work wonders when utilized properly. When Facebook users click on your ad, a form pops up and their contact information from Facebook is automatically entered into the form. You will receive their information and get them started in your sales funnel. Users love this because they never have to leave the site to enter their information, and law firms find it highly beneficial because they can generate leads with little effort.

Create a Lookalike Audience

A lookalike audience on Facebook is an audience that looks similar to your existing customers. If you track your website audience for three months and funnel them to your Facebook page, you may come up with a couple thousand people you can target with ads. Facebook will allow you to create a maximum of 500 Lookalike Audiences from a single source audience.

For example, let's say you installed the pixel on your law firm's website and determined that your best converting leads are men ages 50-55 who live in your city, have children and work full-time jobs. You can target men in a nearby city or state who fit this same demographic in hopes of leading them to your website (or ads) as well.

Creating lookalike audiences is easy because Facebook gives you a step-by-step guide. It even provides helpful tips, such as targeting 1,000 to 50,000 leads, and sourcing your custom audience from your pixel, fans of your page or your mobile app data.

(Facebook's guide to creating a lookalike audience: https://www.facebook.com/business/help/465262276878947)

Note: *There are some specific tricks to refining an audience, so if you have a larger budget or ad spend we would recommend consulting a professional once you have the basics up and running.*

Determine How Ads Work for Your Practice Area

With the Facebook pixel installed, advertising on the site can work well for any practice area. You already know your audience is interested in your services so you can effectively advertise to them. However, if you work in certain areas of practice, you won't be **as** successful with other types of Facebook advertising.

For example, the woman seeking out a divorce may change her relationship status from "**Married**" to "**It's Complicated**." That generates a data point you can use to advertise to her. (I know right – who knew) After some time, she may change her status to "Separated," which is when you can optimize your advertising once again and try to get her to finally convert.

When it comes to a practice area like criminal law, you can't use the same method for reaching your audience. Nobody goes on Facebook and announces they were in jail or committed a crime (hopefully). With criminal law, you'd have to get even more creative. Perhaps you run ads in areas with high amounts of crime. For example, if you're targeting an area where a lot of gun violence occurs, you could create ads that would appeal to people who are dealing with gun charges.

Thinking outside the box is key when it comes to seeing what works for your practice area. Running A/B tests with your ads and measuring your results is going to help you achieve your desired goals.

Keep Your Ads Fresh and Interesting

This is probably the most important item you will read in this blog. FaceBook is not a set it and forget platform. Typically, you'll see the same ads for law firms on television, in newspapers, on Google's search engine results page, on billboards and on the sides of busses. Ad repetition can certainly help when it comes to these avenues. However, on Facebook, your audience is going to quickly burn out on your advertising if you keep showing them the same ad over and over again.

Instead, you should change up your ads weekly in order to keep your audience interested. Make sure the ads are bold and striking. Don't put your logo on the ad, because nobody will know who you are, likely. Also, don't put your picture. Instead, you want to include a visual that is going to get your audience to stop scrolling for a minute and take a look at what you have to offer.

If you specialize in personal injury, your ad may include a photo of a bad car crash, for example. If you are a divorce lawyer, maybe use a photo of two people fighting. Be creative and think about what kind of image would make you want to stop what you're doing and seek out more information. Pro Tip: Be careful not to include overly violent images or those that have blood in them. Aggressive images can be a violation of facebook's policies and can result in your ads being shut down.

See What Mass Tort Marketing Is Already Out There (even if you don't practice in that arena)

Just like on television, mass tort advertising is huge on Facebook. Users are constantly seeing ads for nationwide law firms urging them to act on their asbestos, hernia mesh, medication, Roundup, e-cigarette and bad hip implant issues. If users click on one of these ads, they will be followed around incessantly on Facebook. These nationwide firms are simply generating leads and not even representing these plaintiffs. But even if you aren't looking for these types of cases, take a look at how they market. Look at the visuals, the contact forms and the marketing funnels they use to capture leads.

If you have a smaller firm and you want to capture these

cases, you have an opportunity to grab these leads in the same way and compete for them. You can either work with the mass tort marketers or look to them for guidance on how to set up your own ads. You don't have to have a huge budget to compete in your local market on Facebook. Again, notice how they use strong visuals, have a constant rotation of ads, use compelling language and target the same people over and over.

By putting those same best practices in play, you have the chance to cash in on some of these leads as well. But even if you don't have anything to do with Mass Torts, they are a great source of general technique since the volume is so high from these marketers.

Watch TV?

Another place you can find inspiration for your ads is on television, since it is similar to Facebook advertising; everyone has Facebook and everyone watches TV. Though you don't want to repeat your ads like firms do on TV, you can learn some great advertising lessons from them.

With a TV commercial, you only have 30 seconds to grab someone's attention and make them want to visit your website or pick up the phone and call you. With Facebook, you have even less time, since users are quickly scrolling through their feeds. What can you do to grab someone's attention with a visual, a headline or a video? What can you say that would sell someone on your firm? Always remember to put yourself in your audience's shoes and put their needs above your own. Think about what value you can add to their lives, and then create your advertising messages accordingly.

Getting Started with Facebook Ads

Now that you know the best practices for legal Facebook advertising, you can begin to build your campaigns. Remember to track things like your results and cost per lead, and to build sales funnels that make sense for your firm.

Using Google Ads

Google Ads for the legal industry can look slightly different from other industries, mainly due to the fierce competition present in the field. To help you win an edge against your competitors, improve your ad ranking, and connect with relevant leads, you can use these five infallible Ads tips and strategies for your firm's legal marketing. Much like in the SEO section, you may find we use some lingo you haven't seen before. That's okay. If you don't know it, don't worry we have you covered in the appendix section of this book. We leave this here not to talk over your head, but so that you can at least be exposed to it. You might even use this to vette a vendor or marketer you are evaluating.

What do you think of the above?

5 Full-Proof Tips for Using Google Ads for Law Firm Marketing

Tip #1: Be sure to bid higher strategically
There's no denying that the competition in Ads for law firms is fierce, due to which the ad costs and bid rate can rise rapidly. Therefore, to earn top ad rankings and stay competitive, you must bid a bit higher; strategically. In fact at the time of this writing, cost per click and other pricing factors are the highest they have ever been due to search rate fluctuations.

Remember, bidding high on all ad groups may quickly drain your ad budget; hence it is optimal to unearth your most lucrative keywords and bid higher on them. These keywords don't necessarily have to be your highest volume, but instead should be the ad groups that offer the most conversions. As you receive more conversions and clicks, that higher bid will turn even more valuable, and you will be able to rank higher.

Tip #2: Focus on your credibility and reputation in your ads first

Searching for an attorney online is personal. So much so, it has been the butt of jokes in other advertising recently highlighting that search for an attorney shouldn't even be done in public. To many it's a shameful personal endeavor.

Therefore, do whatever you can to put prospective clients at ease and prove that your firm is a safe and reputable option. For this purpose, your ad copy can highlight benefits like:

- Number of cases won
- Free consultations
- Achievements awarded to the firm
- Flat-rate pricing
- Combined years of experience
- The number of attorneys in the firm
- Your 5 star reviews

Tip #3: Perform competitive research and differentiate yourself

As mentioned earlier, the competition for Ads related to the law firm industry is fierce; thus, you must make yourself stand out somehow. Start by performing competitive research on the opposition to differentiate your firm along with keeping the following considerations in mind:

- Create a relevant and actionable CTA (Call To Action)

- Highlight what makes you better a better choice
- Implement all ad extensions you can include call extensions

One piece of vital advice is to not become obsessed with snooping on your competitor. Simply go through their ads and make yours better. Don't click on them thinking you are charging them money. You aren't. Google will figure it out and return it as a credit.

Tip #4: Correctly set up your geotargeting

If you are an attorney in Alaska, you likely are not the ideal fit for a prospective client in New York. Moreover, apart from bidding on location-based keywords such as "aurora defense lawyer," you must also correctly use geotargeting to ensure your ads are shown to viewers in relevant locations. You can configure your geographic coverage in Ads settings a number of different ways. I recommend targeting zip codes, which will allow you to make bid adjustments for those locations based upon performance.

Tip #5: Develop niche campaigns

If your firm has varying audience segments seeking different services, creating niche campaigns can be a great way to go. The more particular and specific your targeting is, the more relevant your ads will be to the individuals who see them - this means more clicks and more results.

Attorneys often have to get creative to find legal solutions for their clients; similarly, and when it comes to Google Ads, you'll require that creativity to propel new leads. With these give infallible Ads tips for law firms, you will attract and connect with relevant traffic, receive more clicks, and outrank competitors.

Part 7:

BONUS

In this section we wanted to provide some bonus material consisting of content and blogs we have written over the years as an agency.

Search Metrics for Law Firm Marketing to Keep Your Eye On

There are many bad actors out there that know law firms are bringing in good money and are ready to pounce to take advantage of that. Having an understanding of some of these metrics can keep you from being preyed upon by those with malicious intentions. It's easy to present some BS metrics and skew information.

In fact, legal marketing is a totally different playing field from traditional marketing or ecommerce marketing. So, what search metrics matter and which are just fluff? How do you determine conversions for law firms?

Bounce Rate

If you're in the marketing industry you know how valuable a good bounce rate is for a website. If you're a lawyer just trying to understand what's what, a bounce rate is a metric found in Google Analytics. It is a term used in web traffic representing the percentage of visitors who visit your website and then leave after viewing only one page on your site rather than clicking off to view other pages on your website.

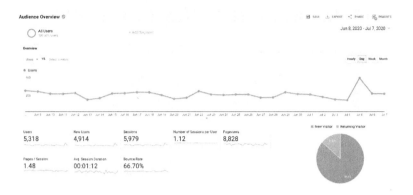

In the above image we can see that over the last month there were 5,318 users and of those 5,318 users 66.7% of them clicked off of the website after viewing only one page. These numbers are pretty normal for a law firm.

A high bounce rate is not a good thing and is usually indicative that a website's home page or landing page aren't relevant to your visitors or that your website isn't user friendly. A common misconception is that a high bounce rate can lead to a lower ranking in the search engines. The truth is the bracket for a "good" bounce rate will vary based on the industry. For law firms, bounce rates tend to average between 50 to 70 percent.

The fact is when people look for legal services, it's kind of like when you buy a car. They're doing a little bit of research first and then they're making a decision. The stats are out there that people look at 3-4 attorneys online before making a choice, so you see that pop up in the metrics. You see a high bounce rate; you see time on site of one and a half to two minutes. People just don't spend a lot of time researching, they try to solve their problem quickly.

Well, we're not an e-commerce business so our conversion rate is very different. One of the things that's unique about law firms is you can never really go into Google Analytics and set up a conversion goal that has any dollar amount attached to it. To a lot of people, that's a totally foreign concept. How do you measure ROI? You measure ROI by being communicative with your client trying to find out who of their leads turns into a case. So, I think that's unique in our business. We spend a lot of time with our clients educating them on what a conversion is and how to follow that conversion path from an SEO perspective all the way down into a law firm business perspective.

How Do Law Firms Measure Conversions?

Conversions for law firms aren't going to measure the same way as traditional marketing likes to determine. You're not going to find accurate conversion rates in your Google Analytics account for your law firm as you're not (normally) selling anything through your website. So, how do you measure conversions for law firms - or any other similarly positioned business in the services industry?

The answer to this comes down to communication between the marketing agency and the client. Well, that and a few other services. Precision Legal Marketing offers clients a live chat service in addition to call tracking services. Many law firms are turning to offering chat services on their website, but where does it go? Are they talking to a human when they chat? What do those representatives say to the leads? Similarly, the call tracking feature allows your marketing team to see how people are finding your law firm, allowing further conversion analysis.

There are a lot of innovative ways in which you can measure conversions for law firms, but without having good communication with your client, it's all kind of a stalemate.

Keywords and Search Engine Ranking

Many law firms understand the volume of a blog section. It's a way of continuing to build on those valuable keywords to drive your website to a coveted top position in the search engines, like Google. When someone queries "divorce lawyer in Virginia Beach", where will your family law practicing law firm show up? Page one or page 10? Many users won't go past page one and if they do, statistics show they don't typically go past page three.

What is the overall goal to search engine ranking though? To drive traffic. It's not enough to simply rank well on the search engines, you want those rankings to drive traffic to your website and hopefully convert those users to clients.

Are you ranking for keywords that your potential clients are actually using?

During COVID-19, the legal industry saw spikes in domestic violence, divorces, child support issues for those facing financial hardship as well as child custody disputes, to name a few. What happens if the parent who has full custody was a healthcare worker on the frontlines of the pandemic? By answering questions that users were actually searching for several law firms were able to find a huge increase in traffic during all of this.

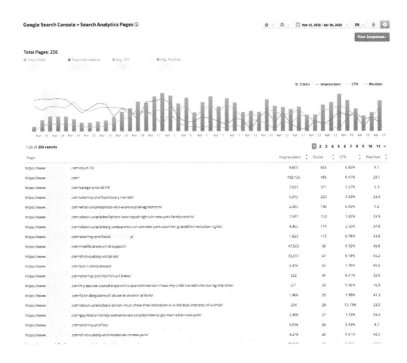

Page	Impressions	Clicks	CTR	Position
https://www. .com/covid-19/	9,603	655	6.82%	9.7
https://www. .com/	102,126	485	0.47%	29.1
https://www. .com/category/covid-19/	7,037	371	5.27%	9.3
https://www. .com/attorney-profiles/steve-j-mandel/	6,312	223	3.53%	23.4
https://www. .com/what-circumstances-void-a-prenuptial-agreement/	2,265	146	6.45%	7.2
https://www. .com/about-us/articles/fathers-have-equal-rights-in-new-york-family-courts/	7,597	123	1.62%	33.9
https://www. .com/about-us/articles/grandparents-can-ask-new-york-court-for-grandchild-visitation-rights/	4,465	114	2.55%	24.8
https://www. .com/attorney-profiles/d y/	1,623	110	6.78%	43.6
https://www. .com/modifications-child-support/	47,503	58	0.12%	45.8
https://www. .com/child-custody-visitation/	33,011	47	0.14%	45.2
https://www. .com/pet-custody-issues/	2,476	42	1.70%	40.6
https://www. .com/attorney-profiles/felicia-l-boles/	522	34	6.51%	32.6
https://www. .com/my-spouse-custodial-parent-is-quarantined-can-i-have-my-child-live-with-me-during-this-time/	371	34	9.16%	16.9
https://www. .com/false-allegations-of-abuse-in-divorce-actions/	1,460	29	1.99%	41.3
https://www. .com/about-us/articles/a-parent-must-show-that-relocation-is-in-the-best-interests-of-a-child/	204	28	13.73%	23.0
https://www. .com/gay-lesbian-family-law/same-sex-couples-how-to-get-married-in-new-york/	2,408	27	1.13%	26.0
https://www. .com/attorney-profiles/	6,016	26	0.43%	8.7
https://www. .com/child-custody-and-mediation-in-new-york/	4,279	26	0.61%	42.5

Ranking for keywords can be challenging. Broad keywords such as "divorce lawyer" can be difficult to rank for - especially as a smaller, local law firm.

The key thing to keep in mind for anybody out there, either in the SEO business or small business owners listening, that these keywords that we're playing with are extremely difficult to rank for. So as a local law firm owner, you have to wade in the same water as all the other big fish. It's this small law firm and the medium-sized local law firm that may have three, four, or five offices. If you're a solo guy sitting up the street in your 2000 square foot office, you've got to compete against the depth and breadth of that law firm. And that's really difficult because they're all the same keywords.

Optimize It or Disavow It

In marketing for the legal sector, there's a right way and a wrong way. The wrong way could get your website flagged as "spammy" causing you to face penalties with the search engines. In fact, it's possible for your Google My Business listing to get flagged as spammy and with everything that's going on right now with the economy, it could take around 45 days for your account to be unsuspended. It is 100% worth it to do things right the first time.

After a law firm has been burned by a marketing agency who charged a fortune but delivered very little, it can be difficult to show them that there is value in marketing - when done correctly.

I can't tell you how many situations I've been in where we'll get called in to consult and it's the same old thing. They're looking for an SEO agency and they want a top-down analysis of what they have. So we look at what they've been doing in the past and we show them a back-link report, we show them traffic metrics, and we're really digging under the hood. They have no idea. And it's not their fault. Mordy, we're like doctors. We're doing a CT scan on their website. So sometimes you have to have tough conversations with folks.

SEO vs. SEM: What's the Difference?

In this book we have laid our tips for both of these practices. But which should you prioritize more?

As marketing has evolved over the years, so too has the language that marketers use. They are all guilty of tossing around acronyms and jargon that often leave the readers confused. And if we are completely honest, many marketers are probably confused about what specific acronyms and terms mean half the time! If you're asking yourself *"what is the main difference between SEO and SEM"*, you're not alone.

The two acronyms and terms that are often interchangeably used without a clear understanding of how they are related and how they differ in meaning are Search Engine Optimization (SEO) and Search Engine Marketing (SEM). They both have a symbiotic relationship, and, when leveraged to their full potential, they can produce *remarkable* marketing results.

Continue reading to learn about *"what is the main difference between SEO and SEM"* and how they each allow marketers to rank pages and increase traffic.

What is the Main Difference Between SEO and SEM?

Search engine optimization, commonly known (and referred to) as SEO, has conventionally been considered an SEM component, i.e., search engine marketing, encompassing both organic and paid tactics. However, today SEM refers exclusively to paid search - meaning you're paying to have your content displayed higher on the search engines.

Search engine optimization is defined as the process of attracting and receiving more traffic from *organic*, free, natural, and editorial results. On the other hand, search engine marketing is getting website traffic through purchasing ads for search engines, think Google's Pay-Per-Click (PPC) ads.

In short, SEO is an organic and free search strategy, whereas SEM is a paid strategy. Both of these strategies must be a part of your law firm's online search marketing arsenal.

SEO Overview

We talked about the basics of SEO in an earlier portion of the book, but here's a quick refresher.

Search engine optimization disciplines the need to constantly evolve to keep up with the ever-changing algorithms of Google. The one constant in SEO is that it's made up of off-page and on-page (i.e., off-site and on-site activities), and these are its two main pillars. We would be remiss if we did not also mention local SEO though (even though we covered it just a couple of chapters ago).

Features of On-Page SEO

- Social sharing integration with content
- Optimized page speed
- Optimized meta details such as page title tag, heading tags, meta descriptions, and image alt name that involve target keywords
- Optimized and well-written page content via strategic keyword research

- Well-formatted and simple page URLs with selective keywords

Features of Off-Page SEO

- Attracting attention from social bookmarking bsites like Digg, Reddit, and Stumbleupon
- Social signals, for example, enhancing traffic to a site from social media sharing
- Building links to attract and acquire quality inbound links

Create high-quality and valuable content useful for your target audiences, such as articles, blog posts, and web page copy. Doing this will allow you to establish your authority which will eventually and ultimately result in increased organic traffic, enhanced opportunities for inbound links, and *more conversions*.

Make sure to pay attention to these off-page and on-page tactics to ensure your web copy, landing pages, blog posts, and articles are optimized for search.

SEM Overview

Search engine marketing (SEM) strictly comprises earning search visibility via paid advertisements on search engine platforms like Google. These paid advertisements are commonly known as PPC or pay-per-click ads. There are several other words used for SEM activities such as paid search advertising, paid search ads, cost per click, or CPC ads.

PPC advertising allows marketers to target potential buyers through keywords and relevant ad copies that match their search requests. These ads show up in SERPs, also known as search engine results pages next to organic listings.

PPC ads allow businesses to increase the visibility of their landing pages, web pages, articles, blog posts, and more.

Examples of SEM Strategy

Google AdWords is, by far, the most popular and widely used search engine platform for hosting ads. There are other platforms as well, such as Yahoo search ads, Bing ads, etc. Whichever platform you select to spend your online marketing budget on, make sure you follow some successful SEM strategies to reap adequate benefits. A few of these strategies include:

1. Generate ad campaigns with a particular audience in mind

2. Create ad groups that comprise of target keyword variations

3. Create relevant ad copies using selective keywords

4. Set a budget for ads

5. Monitor metrics like impressions, clicks, average CPC and click-through rates

There are few other considerations for launching and maintaining a successful paid search ad campaign, but these five are most critical for beginners.

3 Types of Search Engine Marketing

The types of search engine marketing can be characterized into three types:

Search Engine Optimization (SEO)

SEO is a method of enhancing the rankings of a website in the SERPs to drive traffic, achieve more visibility, and eventually help a website grow its leads and conversions.

Search engines like Bing, Yahoo, Google aren't paid to provide ranking in SERPs. Instead, SEO experts offer guidance to optimize a page and make it rank organically.

Search Engine Advertising

While SEO is the way to enhance sites ranking on the SERPs organically; Search engine advertising is the way search engines are paid to make an ad appear on top of their search results. They usually appear on top of the SERPs, above the organic results, and are labeled with an 'AD' tag.

Paid Submission

One of the less common types of search engine marketing is paid submissions. This is a method of listing a business's information, including its site, to online directories through monetary payments. Online directories have editors that manually review the submission, and once approved, these submissions are listed permanently. It can help increase a business's online citation that can affect visibility on search engines.

SEO vs. SEM: Which is Better?

Advocates for either could reason one is more effective and successful than the other. But, we like to see high-quality SEO as an underpinning for high-quality SEM and visa versa. *Both hold significant value and should be part of any inbound marketing strategy.*

Focus on SEO When:

As discussed above, SEO lays the foundation for SEM through optimized content that is useful and attractive for customers. Without web pages, blog posts, articles, and landing pages optimized for search, all SEM efforts would, unfortunately, fail due to poor quality. Additionally, SEO is less expensive over the long term and helps law firms to enhance their search credibility.

SEO is great for building organic rank on the search engines to help drive traffic *organically* to your website over the long haul. Seo takes time to build, and the longer you are at it, the better your results become. Once you achieve top ranking on top keywords, your traffic begins to logarithmically increase.

Focus on SEM When:

If you're launching your website and want to create your initial online footprint to promote a service or product, then SEM would be a good means to receive immediate visibility until you attain organic credibility. An effective PPC campaign can make this happen, but make sure that you do not rely heavily on paid ads in the long run. Quality content is a must for engaging customers to your website and to achieve conversions.

SEM is also great for building brand awareness if you're just getting started, because remember: if people don't know you exist, they won't become customers.

The differences between SEO and SEM are many, but to know when and how to use each is the key to achieving an effective marketing strategy. If your budget allows, coupling SEO and SEM efforts can posture your firm for growth.

Still confused?

You're not alone. It's a confusing topic. My best advice as with anything in this book is to work within a budget and do as much as you can afford. Grow these efforts as you can afford. Remember marketing is a 100% tax write off so invest in your business. Treat SEO as a long term investment and SEM as a short term one. SEM, when configured properly, can be an immediate hit of traffic and cases with measurable ROI (return on investment). SEO is an investment that pays off down the road.

What Happened to the Yellow Pages? Yellow Pages v. Digital Marketing Why Digital Marketing is Now Best

Before technology took over, everyone relied on the yellow pages when they needed something. Believe it or not, in some areas of the country going digital can still be up for conversation. Some of you reading this may not yet have a website, and that's okay. But it's time...

Need a plumber? Find it in the yellow pages!

Need a dentist? Yellow pages lists several!

Need a lawyer? Yup, you guessed it – yellow pages!

But times have changed. Technology is here, making our lives a bit easier. The internet can make a major impact for literally any business, especially a law firm. Did you know 78% of consumers shopping for legal services start their search online?

Attorneys – **just like you** – are still only relying on the yellow pages. While that could certainly still bring in some leads for you, it doesn't even compare to what digital marketing can do for you.

As a lawyer, you can be a bit skeptical of digital marketing because all you have known was yellow pages – and that's okay.

How are the Yellow Pages Like Internet Marketing for Attorneys?

Exposure

You will gain exposure in both. Essentially, they're both the same thing ... sort of.

In YP you bought an ad and it's size and seniority determined it's position. If you weren't far enough up front with a big ad, your response suffered. Not with online marketing. You can pin-point the target of *where* you want to be, when you want to be there.

Available at Their Fingertips

When someone is in need of a lawyer, they can pick up a phone book and start flipping through the yellow pages. They can also go to Google and type in "lawyer in (certain city, state)" and your business will appear IF you are consistent with digital marketing.

Not only that, but if their location is on, their phone *knows* where you are. For example, if they type "divorce lawyers near me", your website and location will be provided in the relevant search results. As an attorney that is marketing on Google, this is a huge advantage due to the fact you can target that user directly.

Easy to find

With the Yellow Pages, you used to let your fingers do the walking, and you went to the lawyer heading. But then you had to go find a phone, which took more time (let's be honest, people get distracted and probably forgot to call by the time they even remembered to grab the phone!)

With digital marketing, all you do is pull your phone out

of your pocket, make a quick search, and dial or click to call. It's easier than ever!

How is Online Marketing Better Than the Yellow Pages?

Now that you have a better understanding of how the yellow pages are similar to internet marketing, let's dive into how this form of marketing can literally *explode* your ROI more than the Yellow Pages could.

Exposure

Let's go back to exposure. In the yellow pages, sure you get exposure but only if someone feels like reading down a whole list of company names. There are several law firms in each area, so yours isn't going to stand out unless you pay even more for a larger ad placement. In today's world, you will only get noticed if someone actually picks up the phone book ... most people toss theirs in the trash.

With digital marketing, you can have more exposure for a better ROI.

Here are just a few ways you can gain exposure with digital marketing

- Google Ads- An ad that appears on the top part of search engine results of Google.
- Facebook Ads– An ad that you can customize so it can reach a specific audience and it will show up in Facebook newsfeed or messenger.
- Social media marketing – Marketing on social media platforms to grow your audience with the end goal of promoting your service.
- Live Chat – A live chat on your website that is available when you're not to answer specific questions.

- Website content with specific keywords used (think headlines in the yellow pages. Those are the keywords that will drive leads to your website from google)
- Google My Business (This one is free = bonus leads!)
- Blog content to gain trust with current and potential leads
- YouTube videos
- Search Engine Optimization (SEO) – Specific keywords that people are searching. We research those keywords carefully and tie them into your content so your target audience can find you easier.

Available at Their Fingertips

Anyone can pick up a phone book and they will see your name if they keep reading, but chances are many won't even own a phone book to begin with.

With digital marketing, you are literally at their fingertips. All they have to do is type in attorney with a city and state, push enter, and there you are — IF you have a good digital marketing strategy in place (don't worry about the strategy, we got you covered.)

Once they find you on Google, they can even call you with the touch of a button if they are on their smartphone.

Easy to Find YOU

Being easy to find goes back to being present on Google and other platforms. Many people use Facebook to find what they need as well. If you are active on Facebook and have reviews, they will be more apt to reach out to you.

Digital marketing makes it convenient and easy to gain immediate trust with your potential new clients. When someone is flipping through the yellow pages, they aren't always sure who to reach out to. With digital marketing, they have reviews and all sorts of information in an instant.

As you can see, internet marketing is like a whole other world when it comes to marketing your legal services. It's more targeted, it creates more potential, and you can grow your firm easier and faster. Of course, you don't have to do this all on your own.

Don't Fall for Those Digital Marketing Scare Tactics

Have you ever heard of the "squeeze" or getting "bumped" from first page search results on Google?

What about hearing that organic traffic is bringing in less traffic than it used to? Or the always famous "I can get you to page 1 in the maps pages on your choice of keywords in less than 30 days or you pay nothing".

Although not entirely incorrect, these phrases are often utilized by some Digital Marketing Agencies that exploit this verbiage to scare you into obtaining their services. They prey on your lack of knowledge and utilize scare tactics to get your business. Rather than being scared, you need to be armed with the right information to combat some of these common misconceptions.

So, let's address what is really being discussed with these scare tactics and how to properly address them.

First, and let's be honest here, this space has always been SUPER competitive with aggregators like Avvo, Laywers. com, Superlawyers and Justia taking up a large percentage of top search engine placement. They own the top of page one in many cases online.

Obtaining a first page ranking can be a challenge when all you focus on are clever "tricks" that attempt to fool Google. However, Google regularly updates their search engine algorithms and their focus has always been to promote quality content. Utilizing clever tips or tricks are typically a short term solution rather than a means to provide long-term growth.

Also consider that Google DOES rule the search world. It's like the British Empire...but remember: You don't poison the King, or his army will strike. When this happens Google will push a sites ranking down well below first page ranking. So, it's good to understand time-tested Google recommended methods to obtain traffic from their search engine.

To improve the level of traffic to your site through organic means is still very much possible. In fact we have increased some of our clients by more than 100% in organic traffic through appropriate means. To do this you NEED to rank for the keywords best associated with your Firm. For example, if you are a divorce attorney, you will NEED to rank for such common phrases like "Divorce Lawyer, Divorce Attorney and "near me" as top keyword examples.

But, that isn't the only step that you'd need to take in order to get quality traffic coming to your site and having customers call your phone.

You'll also need to do the following:

1. Have a SOLID local SEO and map pack ranking. Addressing both search and Google Maps will take a more comprehensive approach to your SEO digital marketing efforts.

2. Work with a certified Google partner who puts an emphasis on local SEO so that you can combat the big boys in your city. Certified Google partners have the latest information on Google best practices that will benefit your firm.

3. Find smaller GEO's to rank in. This is often an over-looked but valuable note... to plan out and execute. For example, say you have an office in Fairfax, VA and you rank well there. But what about ranking well in Tysons or Vienna? With mobile and geo keyword searches you have a shot at beating these big dudes to first page ranking.

The process of addressing these scare tactics is as simple as learning to play with the big boys, including the big aggregators such as Avvo, lawyers.com, Superlawyers and Justia.

Like a financial portfolio, it's good to diversify your efforts by having accounts on each site while you are expanding your digital marketing efforts.

Once you know that marketing is a well-planned out process, scare tactics will never phase you and your digital marketing efforts.

5 Key Marketing Must-Do's and Tips for Lawyers

Is this you? Last year, your marketing campaigns for your law firm didn't turn out exactly as you had hoped. You couldn't reach your KPIs, fulfill your goals or make enough money to justify the time and energy you put into your strategy.

You aren't exactly sure what went wrong – perhaps you didn't understand your audience, you weren't tracking campaigns properly or you didn't hire the right people to help you – but you do know one thing: *this* year, you have to improve.

Thankfully, modern day marketing presents a multitude of ways to reach your target customers and drive conversions for your law firm. It's a confusing landscape out there, and we exist to help clear that up. Whether you are a DIY'er, have an in hour marketing person at your firm or buying marketing services from a vendor, following up on these 5 tips will add to your marketing success.

Here are five marketing tactics to add to your law firm's marketing success.

1. Correctly Set Up Your Google My Business Listing

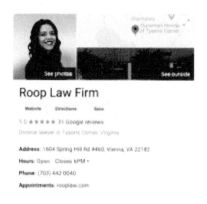

This is number one for a reason. It's the simplest, easiest thing you can set up for your law firm. If you have a GMB listing setup already, make sure you log into it now and ensure you are taking advantage of all the new features. Make sure you have primary and secondary business categories selected, bio and images updated as well as hours and more. Once you log in, migrate to the info tab and fill out every section you possibly can.

Google churns out algorithm updates all the time and many times, they end up shaking up local SEO listings. The businesses that come out on top are ones that listed relevant categories to their businesses on Google My Business as well as included the same or similar keywords on their websites. For example, if you were a personal injury lawyer, you would list that as your primary category and create content around this topic on your site's blog, as well as use those keywords on your home and service pages.

In addition, due to Google's updated neural matching, it doesn't matter whether or not your business type is in your business name anymore. For example, you don't need to list "Matthew and Smith, Personal Injury Lawyers." You could just list "Matthew and Smith" if that's your real business name. Now, Google is now smart enough to tie your keyword and category "personal injury lawyer" to your title, which makes for a better search experience for the user.

To stand out on the search engine results page make sure you completely fill out your profile – including the categories section – and ensure the information is consistent with your website, your Yelp page, and any other business listings you have online. One tool you should consider investing in to guarantee accuracy across the board is BrightLocal, which monitors all your listings and allows you to update them from a simple, easy-to-use dashboard.

2. Increase Your Website Speed

Desktop and mobile website speed has become increasingly important over the years, as Google has changed its algorithm to favor fast sites and users' attention spans have dwindled. According to one study, 53% of mobile users will exit a website that doesn't load within three seconds. Since smartphones account for 70% of time spent with digital media, you need to make sure your law firm site loads especially fast on mobile.

You can do a Website Speed Test, which shows you how many seconds it takes your site to load in different locations around the world. Then, see if those numbers are higher or lower than three seconds. If it takes longer, you'll need to up your speed. How? Compress your HTML,

<u>JavaScript and CSS files</u> (ask your developer about this if you're not technical), don't use too many link redirects, compress your JPG and PNG images and allow your site to be cached just once per year.

3. Utilize Facebook Lead Ads and Google Form Ads

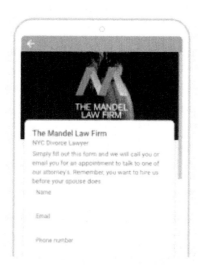

No, we're not talking about traditional PPC. We are talking about products Google and Facebookhave rolled out called lead forms. These ads are meant to keep searchers on the platform they were searching or seeing ads on without having to leave. As such, these types of ads tend to have a cheaper cost per result. If you advertise on Google or Facebook, you want to collect possible clients' information, like their email, phone number and legal needs when they respond to your ads. With these ads, it takes any inadequacy of your website out of the equation. Google and Facebook make it easy by populating users'

information in these forms when they click on your ads. Through these ads, you can generate high-quality leads that will hopefully result in cheaper cost conversions. This year, don't just show your potential customers ads; allow them to click on the ads and fill out a customized form without ever leaving the Facebook or Google platform.

4. Create Local Content and Have Local Se Structure On Your Website

Google pushes content that is local to a user to the top of the search engine results page, because it helps that user find the exact information they need. Local content should be one of your top SEO priorities. This will mean writing content specifically for geographies your firm attracts clients from.

For instance, if you have a blog on your law firm site and run a personal injury law firm in Austin, Texas, you would want to create blog posts like, "What to Do if You're Injured in a Car Accident in Texas" or "What Are Workers Comp Laws in Austin, Texas?" Create location-specific service pages as well, like Personal Injury in Texas or Texas Car Accident Lawyer.

You can use geo targeting to see where most of your website visitors are coming from, and then create content based on that. Another trick is to do keyword research to increase your chance of landing at the top of the search engine results page. Use tools like Moz and SEMrush to find keywords to insert into your blog posts and service pages.

5. Invest in Next Generation Hyper-Targeted Advertising

The old way to advertise to people was to create an ad that was so general it could appeal to a wide range of potential customers. Today, on the other hand, we are generating so much data on our devices that companies can use it to create hyper-targeted ads that actually speak to us and may persuade us to buy a product. You can utilize hyper-targeted ads to find clients as well.

Be as specific as possible when running advertising campaigns. For example, if you're using Facebook ads, don't target a general audience – target a niche one. Don't just say, "males over 30," say, "males between 30-4- in Austin, Texas who like The Home Depot's fan page." Install the Facebook Pixel on your site to target specific users who found you on the social media site or on Google. Look at website data from Google Analytics to find out exactly who your audience is. There's a plethora of data out there; you just need to know how to effectively utilize it to advertise to your potential clients.

6 Ways Your Firm May Be Losing Money

When a law firm hires a legal marketing agency, they should get measurable results that are clear and concise to understand. However, this is not often the case, and your firm may be losing revenue as a result.

When addressing your firm's digital marketing, you only get out of it what you put into it. The sad reality is most of these so-called SEO agencies may offer SEO, content, or link building services for less than $1,000 per month, but the results of their efforts often fall short of expectations, leaving you and/or your firm searching for another SEO agency every 6-8 months.

Let's focus on stopping this cycle so if you're looking for one, you can find a marketing agency that will work with you in getting measurable results and be satisfied with your investment. *cough* Precision Legal Marketing *cough*

Here are 6 ways your firm is losing revenue through digital marketing:

1. More than just a Pretty Website

It's great having a website that looks fantastic but having a pretty website doesn't make you money because no one knows it's there.

This often happens because an attorney or law firm may hire a fantastic web developer, and they will get the site that they want because the web developer is good at his job. But web developers usually are not SEO or marketing experts.

The reason is web developers typically don't:

- Write or Edit content for a website, such as a blog.
- Stay up-to-date on best SEO practices, including but not limited to…
  - Link Building/Outreach
  - Audit/Analyze and Diagnose/Repair the On-Site SEO of a website.
- Experience in digital marketing, especially for a law firm.
- The ethical concerns with various state bars. For example, in Texas you have to submit your site for full approval to the bar.

But basic on-page Search Engine Optimization is never enough to be competitive, especially when your firm is competing with hundreds of others in your area.

How to reduce your loss in revenue:

When hiring a marketing agency, they should be able to share:

- Examples of their SEO success through case studies of their clients.
- Demonstrate clearly how SEO improved search engine visibility, increase in website traffic and phone calls, along with specific keyword rankings over time for their clients.
- Actual Data from an analytics tool such as Google Analytics, and be able any questions to where you can understand them.

While having a great looking website is nice, just remember that alone is not SEO.

Having a Legal Marketing Agency that works with designers (or have their own) will help you reduce the potential of your Law Firm in needing to find a new agency every few months because you're not getting the results you need in improving website traffic or acquiring leads.

2. Managing your Digital Marketing Expectations

If you spend up to $10,000 a month in ad spend on Facebook, how do you know you are getting what you paid for?

Many agencies will send screenshots of their Google Analytics reports and highlight the metrics that put the results in the best light. But often attorney's don't know what these screenshots or reports mean as they either the reports are vague, or more importantly the attorney doesn't even have a clue as to what the agency does every month.

Not understanding basic reporting from an agency is not understanding where your money is going. If an agency doesn't manage this expectation by answering your questions and making sure you understand what is going on, it may be time to search for a new agency to manage your digital marketing efforts.

How to reduce your loss in revenue:

Having a report that you understand is paramount in helping you reign in the cost associated with your business.

A digital marketing agency should help you understand what any report is saying and help you feel at ease while they help you through the entire SEO process.

From doing a digital audit and providing recommendations,

the agency should be able to show and explain what needs to be done every step of the way and have your trust in making those recommendations happen.

3. Marketing is Metrics

With all this money invested each month into your digital marketing efforts, how do you know it's actually working?

A Digital Marketing Agency does this by setting up the metrics to 'track' the results of their efforts. This often includes adding some code to landing pages, websites, etc... in order to monitor and report on specific goals.

This is the core of improving your firm's digital marketing efforts that allows the agency to have the evidence they require to make informed decisions.

How to reduce your loss in revenue

By ensuring the proper tracking codes and metrics are in place, you can see what parts of your marketing efforts are actually generating revenue.

For example, by setting up call tracking, you will know if the content you are creating and publishing is increasing calls because the metrics are recording this information.

Tracking conversions like phone calls, live chats and forms being filled out allows for you to not only measure results, but to see how to regularly improve those results. A quality legal marketing agency will address this 'Intake' of information and data, and consistently work with you to actually LOOK at the data and doesn't just sell you on services.

Just know that Marketing is Metrics, and without the information to review, you are just making assumptions.

4. Content is King

Going back to #2, let's manage your expectations...

When hiring an agency to improve your law firms SEO, know that it's nearly impossible to get more traffic to your firm's website without having a comprehensive content strategy in place.

SEO takes work, and there's only so much that can be done with a website that is less than 20 pages, which are MOST law firm sites.

It takes a consistent amount of highly targeted content to obtain an increase in traffic and leads.

How to reduce your loss in revenue

When discussing content, we usually talk about articles or blog posts as part of your website to help drive interest and traffic to your site which should increase client leads.

To address the issue of content marketing, your Law Firm needs to have a content marketing calendar. This calendar should include specific topics associated with your practice, and when to publish those topics. This is part of documenting your content marketing strategy, and without it, you're without a proper strategy to address Search Engine Optimization.

But who will write the content?

Having a quality agency that will take on this responsibility is extremely important.

The competition must be studied, keywords must be researched, a content strategy must be developed and the content must be written.

Keywords are those words and phrases people actually use when searching for something on the internet. Research and developing a keyword list drives the content that is needed for your Firm. In our business, there are few converting keywords... such as Divorce Lawyer, Divorce Attorney and ... near me are the main converting keywords. You may want more Child Custody cases, so tailoring blogs and content to those specific keywords drives the development of your content marketing calendar.

Many law firms prefer lawyers writing content for their website, however the people reading the content most likely will not be lawyers. Rather they are individuals who are seeking a lawyer for their services.

A good marketing agency should be able to work with you in making sure content is written by a qualified individual that speaks to the right target audience while at the same time ensuring that portion of content published is optimized appropriately for search engines.

It should be stated that no matter who writes the content, legal advice shouldn't be given for legal and ethical reasons.

5. Building Links

This is often the most confusing part of digital marketing to a lawyer. It's also the part of SEO that can do more harm than good if done improperly. But having an experienced agency to address this will help you avoid bad and damaging practices.

Search engines, such as Google, rank sites based on their quality and reputation. The algorithm may change each year, but the concept still remains. To get your law firm's site onto the first page of search engine results, not only do you have to have quality content and your website optimized, but other sites that are more reputable than yours need to cite your content as well.

Publishing content and cleaning up on-site SEO are the basics, but sets your firm up for a quality link-building strategy. Not building links aggressively will make it more difficult to compete, especially in the legal industry.

How to reduce your loss in revenue

Building links is all about quality, and the best links are usually earned.

An agency may do outreach or publish link-worthy content, but the goal is to get a link from your website onto a website that is of a similar or related topic. In this regard, it's good to note that an agency can't build all the links you need.

A good agency will be transparent as to what links are being built – and if they are safe or potentially risky.

Knowing where and how your Law Firm is cited on the web will help you market yourself and your firm better.

6. Education Never Ends

The world of digital marketing is always shifting based on latest trends, and a good marketing agency should be willing and able to teach you the latest practices.

Although you may be paying an agency to address all of these items, it's important you have a good concept of how SEO works, and how it can improve your firm's bottom line by providing more website traffic and increasing the number of leads (clients) for your firm.

By staying up to date on latest trends, you should be able to hold your agency accountable for their efforts.

81 FREE Sites to Post Your Press Release

Note: Oftentimes, free distribution sites will **_not_** give you a dofollow backlink, meaning there would be no SEO value/ no backlink to your site that will help improve your Domain Authority. If that is your aim in sending press releases, you may want to consider the paid route. Additionally, if you're relying on the free distribution sites to get you in front of journalists, free may not be the best choice for you. Many of these sites offer a paid/upgrade version if you choose to go that route.

- http://1888pressrelease.com
- http://addpr.com
- http://afly.com
- http://astro-business.com
- http://betanews.com
- http://bignews.biz
- http://bigrockwebdirectory.com
- http://bitboot.com
- http://businessportal24.com
- http://businessservicesuk.com
- http://cgidir.com
- http://clickanews.com
- http://clickanews.net
- http://clickpress.com
- http://dmnnewswire.digitalmedianet.com
- http://signup.ecommwire.com
- http://enewswire.co.uk
- http://emeapr.com
- http://exactrelease.com

- http://express-press-release.net
- http://freepressindex.com
- http://free-press-release.com
- http://free-press-release-center.info
- http://i-newswire.com
- http://information-online.com
- http://it-analysis.com
- http://itbsoftware.com
- http://it-director.com
- http://live-pr.com
- http://mediasyndicate.com
- http://netbizresources.com
- http://netforcenews.com
- http://netforcepr.com
- http://netforcepress.com
- http://netforcetechnology.com
- http://newsactive.net
- http://newsinsites.com
- http://newsphase.com
- http://newswiretoday.com
- http://newsmakers.co.uk
- http://onlineprnews.com
- http://openpr.com
- http://our-newsletter.com
- http://pagerelease.com
- http://pitchengine.com
- http://postafreepressrelease.com
- http://pr80.com
- http://prfire.co.uk
- http://prfree.com
- http://prfriend.com
- http://pr-inside.com
- http://prleap.com

- http://prlog.org
- http://prmac.com
- http://prurgent.com
- http://przoom.com
- http://pr.com
- http://pr9.net
- http://prbd.net
- http://pressabout.com
- http://pressbox.co.uk
- http://pressexposure.com
- http://pressmethod.com
- http://pressreleasecirculation.com
- http://pressreleasesonline.co.uk
- http://update.press-network.com
- http://prfocus.com
- http://pubarticles.com
- http://releasewire.org
- http://sbwire.com
- http://seenation.com
- http://tectrical.com
- http://technifuture.com
- http://technofrantic.com
- http://theopenpress.com
- http://ukprwire.com
- http://upvery.com
- http://usprwire.com

107 Websites to Get Your Law Firm Listed On Now

As a bonus resource, we've put together a list of 107 places you can build a citation (listing) for your law firm. The list below includes the site name, the URL and the site's Domain Authority. The list is sorted by the latter, so start at the top and work your way to the end.

Website	URL	Domain Authority
Google.com	https://www.google.com/	100
maps.apple.com	https://www.apple.com/maps/	100
facebook.com	https://www.facebook.com/	96
yelp.com	https://www.yelp.com/	93
yellowpages.com	https://www.yellowpages.com/	87
angieslist.com	https://www.angieslist.com/	85
findlaw.com	https://www.findlaw.com/	82
manta.com	https://www.manta.com/	80
tomtom.com	https://www.tomtom.com/en_gb/	80
bizcommunity.com	https://www.bizcommunity.com/	76
nextdoor.com	https://nextdoor.com/	76
justlanded.com	https://www.justlanded.com/	75

hg.org	https://www.hg.org/	64
insidenova.com	https://www.insidenova.com/	64
aboutus.com	https://aboutus.com/	64
company.com	https://www.company.com/	59
spoke.com	https://www.spoke.com/	59
yellowbook.com	http://www.yellowbook.com/	59
americantowns.com	https://www.americantowns.com/	59
brownbook.net	https://www.brownbook.net/	59
chamberofcommerce.com	http://chamberofcommerce.com/	58
communitywalk.com	https://www.communitywalk.com/	58
hotfrog.com	https://www.hotfrog.com/	56
local.botw.org	https://local.botw.org/	55
storeboard.com	https://storeboard.com/	55
showmelocal.com	https://www.showmelocal.com/	53
lacartes.com	http://www.lacartes.com/	52
trepup.com	https://www.trepup.com/	52
tupalo.com	http://tupalo.com/	52
hub.biz	http://hub.biz/	51
cybo.com	https://www.cybo.com/	50
ebusinesspages.com	https://ebusinesspages.com/	50
bubblelife.com	https://www.bubblelife.com/	48

yellow.place	https://yellow.place/en/philippines/abaca	48
citysquares.com	https://citysquares.com/	48
2findlocal.com	https://www.2findlocal.com/	47
callupcontact.com	https://www.callupcontact.com/	47
cityof.com	https://www.cityof.com/	47
agreatertown.com	https://agreatertown.com/	46
iglobal.co	https://www.iglobal.co/	46
n49.com	https://www.n49.com/	46
searchonamerica.com	https://www.searchonamerica.com/	46
us.enrollbusiness.com	https://us.enrollbusiness.com/	46
legalreach.com	https://www.legalreach.com/	46
golocal247.com	https://www.golocal247.com/	45
parkbench.com	https://parkbench.com/	45
whodoyou.com	https://www.whodoyou.com/	44
geebo.com	https://geebo.com/	44
trustlink.org	https://www.trustlink.org/tlhome2.aspx	44
lawyerland.com	https://www.lawyerland.com/	42
tuugo.us	https://www.tuugo.us/	42
askmap.net	http://www.askmap.net/	42
bizvotes.com	http://www.bizvotes.com/	42

cityfos.com	https://www.cityfos.com/	42
place123.net	http://www.place123.net/	42
find-us-here.com	https://www.find-us-here.com/	41
opendi.us	https://www.opendi.us/	41
myhuckleberry.com	http://myhuckleberry.com/	40
wherezit.com	http://www.wherezit.com/	39
bizhwy.com	https://www.bizhwy.com/	39
globalcatalog.com	https://globalcatalog.com/	38
fonolive.com	https://fonolive.com/	37
teleadreson.com	https://teleadreson.com/	37
biznet-us.com	https://www.biznet-us.com/	36
justgreatlawyers.com	https://www.justgreatlawyers.com/	35
411.info	https://411.info/	34
akama.com	http://www.akama.com/	34
wand.com	https://www.wand.com/core/default.aspx?redir=1	34
getfreelisting.com	https://getfreelisting.com/	33
travelful.net	http://www.travelful.net/	32
finditguide.com	https://www.finditguide.com/	31
bizidex.com	https://bizidex.com/en	30
intengine.com	https://intengine.com/	26

reviewyourattorney.com	https://www.reviewyourattorney.com/	25
usa-co.com	https://www.usa-co.com/	24
criminallaw.com	https://criminallaw.com/	24
cataloxy.us	https://www.cataloxy.us/	23
us-business.info	https://us-business.info/	23
lawyerdb.org	http://www.lawyerdb.org/	22
courthousesquare.com	https://www.courthousesquare.com/	22
pathlegal.com	https://pathlegal.com/	21
lawdeeda.com	https://www.lawdeeda.com/	21
linkbyme.com	http://www.linkbyme.com/	21
placelookup.net	https://www.placelookup.net/	20
us-info.com	https://www.us-info.com/fr/world	20
alphalegal.com	https://alphalegal.com/	19
Home8.org	http://home8.org/	18
Personal Injury Law Guru	https://www.personalinjurylaw.guru	18
explorelawyers.com	https://www.explorelawyers.com/	17
acompio.us	https://www.acompio.us/	16
legallistings.us	https://www.legallistings.us/	15
lawyersservice.com	https://www.lawyersservice.com/	12
tegfy.com	https://www.tegfy.com/en	11

mapquest.com	https://www.mapquest.com/	89
merchantcircle.com	https://www.merchantcircle.com/	72
elocal.com	https://www.elocal.com/	56
ezlocal.com	https://ezlocal.com/	55
cylex.us.com	https://www.cylex.us.com/	46
expressbusinessdirectory.com	http://www.expressbusinessdirectory.com/	45
find-open.com	https://find-open.com/	31
lawfather.com	http://lawfather.com/	28
myattorneyhome.com	http://myattorneyhome.com/	22
lawreferralconnect.com	http://lawreferralconnect.com/	20
nearfinderus.com	https://nearfinderus.com/	19
ilawconnect.com	https://www.ilawconnect.com/	14
globallawdirectories.com	http://www.globallawdirectories.com/	13
yellow-pages.us.com	https://yellow-pages.us.com/	13
lawyersnear-byme.com	https://ezlocal.com/	<10

Resources

Precision Legal Marketing:
https://precisionlegalmarketing.com/

Legal Marketing Straight Talk:
http://legalmarketingstraighttalk.com/

Legal Marketing Straight Talk Podcast:
https://anchor.fm/legalmarketing

Legal Marketing Straight Talk – Facebook Group:
https://www.facebook.com/groups/
legalmarketingstraighttalk

Facebook Ads for Beginners – Facebook Group:
https://www.facebook.com/groups/
FBAdvertisingForBeginners

Beginner's Guide to Marketing:
https://www.beginnersguidetomarketing.com/

Additional Resources

Moz
https://moz.com/

SEMrush
https://www.semrush.com/

ahrefs
https://ahrefs.com/

RankRanger
https://www.rankranger.com/

BrightLocal
https://www.brightlocal.com/

Hubspot
https://www.hubspot.com/

Facebook for Business
https://www.facebook.com/business

Google's Resources

Google Trends
https://trends.google.com/trends

Google Analytics
https://analytics.google.com/analytics/web/

Google Search Console
https://search.google.com/search-console/welcome

Google Ads
https://ads.google.com/home/#!/

Follow Us on Social Media

Facebook:
https://www.facebook.com/precisionlegalmarketing

Instagram:
https://www.instagram.com/precisionlegalmarketing/

LinkedIn:
https://www.linkedin.com/company/
precision-legal-marketing

Twitter:
https://twitter.com/legalmarketings

YouTube:
https://www.youtube.com/channel/
UCCHTWLY8wtJaS8bRop8z88Q

About Precision Legal Marketing

Precision Legal Marketing

Finally solve the legal marketing puzzle.

Tired of endless law firm marketing failure?

Precision Legal Marketing is an award winning full service marketing agency that exclusively works with attorneys and law firms through the United States and Canada.

We offer future proof web design, industry leading SEO & reporting, paid marketing that delivers real conversions and more.

A one-size-fits-all mentality just doesn't work anymore in law firm marketing consulting. The days of throwing up a <u>website</u> and forgetting about it for a few years are over. From varying social trends to <u>search engine</u> algorithm changes, you have to be on the cutting edge to stay ahead of the curve. We help you achieve that goal. When you hire us you don't just gain a marketing agency, you gain a family. So do we. It sounds cliche, but it really isn't. It's important.

You are taking your business that you have spent years building and entrust us to help you grow it. That comes with a responsibility we take personally. Whether you are a solo practitioner or a AMA Law 100 firm, we take our commitment to your growth and your satisfaction seriously.

We have helped hundreds of law firms across the nation finally solve the legal marketing puzzle.

Author Bio
Steven Long

Steven Long is passionate about helping people succeed. It was this passion that led him to a career as a Law Firm Marketing Consultant at LexisNexis – Martindale Hubbell, and this passion that encouraged him to start the boutique agency, Precision Legal Marketing, in 2014. Steven is President of Precision Legal Marketing, where his influence drives the company's commitment to clients and their marketing strategies.

The field of law firm marketing is unique, and to be successful marketers must understand the initiatives of law firms and the needs of legal clients. Steven has dedicated his career to individualized and poignant legal marketing initiatives. Steven draws on his extensive experience in the field of law firm marketing and a healthy coffee habit to provide interesting and tailored solutions for each legal professional that works with Precision Legal Marketing.

Steven has three favorite hobbies, playing hockey, Formula 1 racing, and going for a drive. These activities highlight the best of his personality, including accuracy, quick assessment of a situation, control, and leadership. All of these traits are apparent in the meaningful work Steven produces for clients. Steven's continued enthusiasm and approach to marketing strategies are embodied in his favorite quote from hockey great, Wayne Gretzky, "We miss 100% of the shots we don't take."

Connect with Steve on LinkedIn:

https://www.linkedin.com/in/steven-long-2860628/

Author Bio
Jessica Ainsworth

Jessica Ainsworth, bestselling author of *The Beginner's Guide to Marketing* book series and founder of <u>Beginner's Guide to Marketing</u> works as the Director of Social Media and Content Marketing for Precision Legal Marketing. She has a strong background in research and analytics and has turned that into a passion for marketing. Jessica loves helping small business owners understand the nuances of the marketing industry helping them to conquer their own mountains - or at least be able to avoid those who may be looking to take advantage of them.

Former intelligence analyst and total nerd, Jessica has a special fondness for research and analytics. Having a strong background in analytics, marketing seemed like an almost natural career transition. She is a veteran, author, marketing professional, philanthropist and board member at 22 March for Life, a veteran suicide prevention organization - and also a super huge comic nerd (living that Webtoons life, yo!).

Connect with Jessica on LinkedIn!

LinkedIn personal:
https://www.linkedin.com/in/jessica-ains-3b3194187/

Acknowledgements

Jyllian for being my rock

Jim & Carol Long, bet you never thought I would do this.

Mark Leader, you would have thought this was pretty cool.

Lu Aloupas our first client.

Steve and Ellen Mandel who are some of the finest people I know.

The entire Precision team, we couldn't do anything with you.

And Jessica who really made this all possible

Sirpriz